To Rosa

The Book on
Retail Site Selection

Slaying the Location
Dragon

to our continued success!

Kelly

Kelly C. Laughton

The Book on Retail Site Selection
Slaying the Location Dragon

www.thedragonbooks.com

Publisher
10-10-10 Publishing
Markham, ON
Canada

Printed in the United States of America and Canada
ISBN: 978-1-77277-152-7

Contents

Dedication

*This book is dedicated to the memory of my brother,
the late Stewart Laughton and my father,
the late Hugh Laughton,*

Love always.

Acknowledgements

My publisher and mentor, Raymond Aaron, and his hard working team at 10-10-10 Publishing, thanks for making this book possible

My ever loving and supportive husband, Lee Downer, & our sassy red tabby cat, "Little Red"

My sister, Colleen Laughton, and her husband, my brother-in-law, David Eryou

My 90 year old and going strong mother, Elsie Laughton

My long-time partner in crime and friend, Gerry Lazar

My bonus chapter author and all round brilliant commercial real estate lawyer, Robert Kligerman

My book cover designer, the talented Amy Barroso of White Lightening Communications

Good friends and supporters, Tekla & Maxwell Nelson and Dr. Charmaine Nelson, McGill University

My daily accountability partner, Myrtle Mitton

Kelly C. Laughton

My virtual support team without whom I would be sunk:
Sherri Pickering, Carrie Pate, Carrie Walkden, Aaron Neilson-Belman

Maz Sharif and his team at Sign-a-Rama

My book architect, Cara Witvoet, my editor, Lisa Browning, Helen Everett, and all the other supportive team members at the Raymond Aaron Group

My virtual office support team at Regus Canada, especially Ehab Hamuda and Harshali Dhotre

My business associates and friends, including Frank Ho, East Star Times/Nations, Tom Lin, Nations Fresh Foods, Lillian Kwok Nations Fresh Foods and Mississauga Chinese Business Assoc.

Jocelyn Mainville, Jackson Square

Phil Richardson and Danielle Papillon, Take the Step Ahead Inc.

Amit and Swapna Ambegaonkar, Your Profound Solutions

Wayne Paterson, Developers and Chains

Jennifer Huntley, Davpart

Loreta DeAllie, Trinity Development

The Book on Retail Site Selection

Avi Behar and all the members of the Behar Group

Greg Rabin, Paracom Realty

Mitch Moss, Crofton Moore

Fred Joseph, Avison Young

Grant Gorchynski, Lori Da Silva, Hitesh Patel, Lisgar Development Ltd.

Kevin Knott, Peter Dhillon and their team at Your Dollar Store with More

Peter Rakovalis and his team at Mary Brown's Chicken

Anabela Santos, Orlando Espanola, and Geeta Ghandi, Sobeys

Sharon Munslow, Street Properties

Dean Wilmot and Robert McKee, Firm Capital

Moshe Batalion, Derek Hogan, Josh Katz and all the other good people at RioCan

My friend and former property manager, Patricia Martin and my friends and former landscapers, Eric and Danielle Gordon

My friends, neighbors and cat sitters for whom we are truly grateful, Anne Schofield and Jessica Huang

Our friends and Danglefit clown troop, Elizabeth Kaczmarek, Gigi Lau, Barbara Heifetz and Pamela Heifetz

My accountant and his team, Milos Hlavacek

My bank manager, Steve Kim, and his team at TD Canada Trust

My mechanics, Mike and Luis and their team that Bertrand Auto

Our veterinarian, Dr. Susan Thomas, The Cat Hospital

My former work mates at Goudy Real Estate, including Len Goudy, Mary Garneau, Michael Pearlman, Cory Rosen, John Amos, Al Lebon, Nancy Chamberlain

My former workmates at Prime Management Group, Christie DeBolt, Peter Tandon, Susie Petrini

My former employers at Staubach, Harry McKeague and Michel Léonard

My former workmates at Blockbuster Video, Terry McGovern, Susan Noble, John Amos, Linda Budd, and many others

The Book on Retail Site Selection

My former work mates at Orlando Corporation, including Ed Nachoff, the late Howard Weinberg, Carlo Fidani, the late Ori Fidani, Dan Hyde, and all the others

My teachers, mentors, friends, and fellow students and warriors in our quest for personal development, through Peak Potentials and New Peaks, now Success Resources, T. Harv Eker, Robert Raymond Riopel, Roxanne Riopel, Michael Silvers, Eric Frady, Lou Altman, Kim Cobb, Marie Cantone, Kent Georgi, Susan Tomlinson, Jacques Godin, The CEO of Music "Rasta", Anick Silencieux, Randi Gitlin Markel, Adam Markel

Werner Lomker Jr, Dominos Empire

Chuck Abou Saab, Kebaberie

Michael Gouveia, Unparallel Brand +Design

Ash & Anil Anand, Crack Me Up

Arash Kamali, Valency

Parisa Javadieram, Salon Parisa

George Kottas, Bite Me Grill, George's BBQ

Stan Siedlikowski, Laura Lalonde, Sherry Dubois, Bruce Henderson, Intercity Shopping Centre

Confederation College, Deborah Kraft, my unrelenting marketing instructor who taught me to hold myself accountable, now Archdeacon Kraft, St. Paul's Anglican Church, thank you Deborah.

Joyce Sharpe, Janet Sharpe and Karen Sharpe (Skochinski), who believed in me and encouraged me to take my first steps in the corporate world.

Miss Vale, my kindergarten teacher at Francis Street Public School, who prepared me for my world debut as a solo artist singing Away in a Manger at First Church United, age 6

And to all my other friends, family, kin folk, teachers, neighbors, co-workers, and loved ones who have taught me and helped me along my journey so far, thank you, I love you.

Kelly

Foreword

If you are in a business that requires a physical place to serve your customers, clients or patients in person, *The Book on Retail Site Selection: Slaying the Location Dragon* is for you. I am excited to tell you that, in this book, Kelly C. Laughton shares with you the secrets of site selection success that are known by the large national retail chains and big restaurant brands. Kelly reveals to you everything you need to know about retail site selection and how to apply it in your business, large or small.

After a career spanning more than three decades, working with retailers and shopping centers, Kelly will take you step by step through the location jungle, to a place of success and prosperity for your business.

The location you choose for your business is a key marketing decision. It affects not only how your client base perceives your business, but also your suppliers, other potential landlords, and the world in general. Your brand will also be significantly affected by the type of real estate you choose.

She wants you to know that, because of your personal connection with your target market and her tools provided in this book, you will be far less vulnerable to the ravages of e-commerce.

Kelly C. Laughton

Follow her formula for successful site search techniques, lease negotiations and location branding to ensure the most successful location and lease for your bricks and mortar business. She will help you *Slay the Location Dragon!*

Raymond Aaron
New York Times Bestselling Author and Real Estate Guru

Your Quest for Success Begins Here...

Congratulations for finding this book. It is a tool to help you place your live and in person business on the path to success and growth.

If you need to meet your customer, client, or patient in person, this book is for you. Yours is a business that requires a bricks and mortar location to personally interact with other people. So that means businesses like services, restaurants, and some types of retail, grocers, and entertainment. And congratulations again because you have chosen a type of business that will not get wiped out by the Internet. Certainly, the Internet will influence how you operate and market your business, but ultimately we all need to be personally present in order to get our teeth cleaned, have our glasses repaired, or meet our pals at the coolest new restaurant for some great food and laughs. After all, you can't get your hair cut on the Internet.

Technology is changing almost every industry so quickly now, that some of the tried and true principles provided in this book will be affected. Recently, I was chatting with one of our restaurant clients and he told me that due to the new UberEATS app, his BBQ take out business, George's BBQ, could now take less square footage and locations with less parking. The daily revenue stream from the UberEATS app pays the rent, labor, and some of the other monthly costs in the first few days of the month.

Become the best you that you can be

I believe in personal development. To me, there are few better ways to spend your hard-earned money than learning to become the best you that you can be. When I started reading and listening to positive books and recordings, and going to live training seminars, my life (and business) started to change for the better. An author by the name of Simon Sinek said, *"People don't buy what you do; they buy why you do it."* Knowing your "why" will make all the difference when the going gets rough.

I also believe in free enterprise. At the age of 18, I got my first sales job where I earned commission only. I sold the advertising and set up the distribution points for a small local magazine called *Cars and Homes Classified*. The more advertising I sold, the more I earned. The more distribution points I set up for the magazine, the greater the circulation and effectiveness of the advertising. I was also the one that went out and took the pictures and wrote the descriptions of all the cars and homes that were advertised for sale in the magazine. And when we got close to the printing deadline, I also helped with the paste up and layout.

It was a fun job and I was fired up. My employers were two entrepreneurial brothers, David and Blair Obourne. Together they owned a web press and printed flyers for grocery stores, the local weekly tabloid, and all sorts of other web press printing. If it weren't for their entrepreneurship, there would not have been a job for me. Thanks, David and Blair.

I needed wheels to get around and I didn't yet own a car so when I had to go on sales calls, Blair would lend me his white Corvette that had a high-performance engine. Now you know why I liked my job so much! One day, I took it out on the highway to see how fast it would go, and guess what? I got busted. The police officer must have been amused, though, because he didn't even give me a speeding ticket. That was the job where I began to learn about business and advertising and how they work.

So why did I write this book?

Small businesses are the backbone of our economy. In North America, statistics clearly show that the vast majority of new jobs are created by small business. So, when governments ease the burden or create incentives for small business, that's when economies really start to flourish and grow.

After three decades of working with retailers and shopping centers, I've learned a lot about what works and what doesn't work. When I meet people wanting to lease a retail space for their business, it doesn't take me long to know who will even qualify to lease the space, let alone who will have a successful business.

Back to my story... fresh out of college, I got hired as the first ever Marketing Director for the newly built, big, enclosed mall in my hometown of Thunder Bay. That's in Northwestern Ontario, Canada's gateway to the west and the head of Great Lakes. It was my job to attract customers to the shopping center. We had a great operations team, and most days were really exciting. We did sales promotions, advertising, public relations, home shows, car shows, fashion shows, fund raisers, Toys for Tots, Photos with Santa, Photos with the Easter Bunny, (guess who had to wear the Easter Bunny costume when the costume kid didn't show up?), Breakfast with Santa, Sidewalk Sales, radio remotes, Antique Car Shows, Mother's Day, Father's Day, Back to School, Valentine's Day, and the list goes on. There was something going on in the shopping center pretty much every week.

An entrepreneurial developer by the name of Robert Campeau built that shopping center. In the 1980s, he led a company that was building shopping centers right across Canada. If it weren't for his entrepreneurship, I would not have had a job. In fact, that shopping center created hundreds of jobs directly, and thousands of jobs indirectly.

In addition to the anchor stores, there were about 200 retail stores, services, and restaurants that made up the CRU (commercial retail unit) tenants. Some were national chains, some were franchises (with local franchisees), and some were independent retailers from the surrounding city. The shopping center was like a business incubation lab. I knew every store owner or store manager by name and did my best to get all the merchants to participate in all mall promotions and events. The degree of success of each business, I learned, depended upon its business plan and how well the store manager and store staff worked their business plan in conjunction with the mall's marketing plan. They did not have to worry about their location. Their business was located in the strongest and most productive retail property within an eight-hour driving radius.

Typical of a regional shopping center, monthly sales were collected from each tenant. The ones with the highest sales in their respective categories were usually the national chains with the well-known brands. Their store managers were incentivized and had a clearly defined sales goal for each month. The next level of performance came from the franchised businesses; however, this was not always the case because franchises can be strong or weak, depending on the operator, as well as the franchise itself. Usually at the bottom of the sales performance chart were any independent retailers. I remember walking through the shopping center one day, and I noticed two of the independent storeowners standing in the common area complaining to each other that there was no traffic in the mall. Meanwhile, there were customers in their respective stores with no one serving them.

I don't want to target independent retailers. They are what adds spice to a shopping center. There is a problem in the shopping center industry called *shopping center sameness,* which means having the same mix of national retailers and restaurants in every mall. Independent retailers make shopping malls more interesting. But the problem is, many owner operated retail stores never manage to generate the sales volume needed to stay long term in the big enclosed malls. But nonetheless, that mall managed to achieve the highest sales per square foot in the whole company on several occasions, even beating the productivity of malls in much bigger cities. I am proud to say we also won two international marketing awards from the International Council of Shopping Centers (I.C.S.C.).

Hot Spots – did it matter where the business was located in the mall?

By using the mall's leasing plan, we would make a color chart of all the retailers' sales performance levels. Top performers were colored bright red, and then the next levels were colored pink, orange, yellow, green, and blue for the lowest levels of sales performance. It allowed us to see if there were any areas in the shopping center where all the stores in one area or another were suffering. That was not the case. Our analysis showed that it did not matter much where the business was located within the shopping center. Higher and lower performers were evenly disbursed. From what we observed, the things that made the difference were the strength of the brand, the store management and staff team, and the customer experience.

I am passionate about helping you set your business up in the right location. I recently heard a speaker say that for every new millionaire, one hundred new jobs are created. In 2012, according to US Census Bureau data, there were 5.73 million employer firms, and businesses with less than 20 workers that made up 89.6% of those. As well, small businesses account for more than 98% of all firms in Canada and proportionally play a large role in job creation, creating 77.7% of all private sector jobs from 2002 to 2012. That means that the strength of our economies and countries is dependent upon the success of small business. And that's one of the reasons why I want you to see you succeed.

Setting your business up in the right place puts you on the road to success. I see so many people, both new and experienced in business, that come to us without any idea what they expect to do in sales or what their proposed business can afford to pay in rent. It is a good idea to find out what market rents are prior to writing your business plan. But other than learning market rents, searching for a location for your business comes at the end of the business start-up process, not the beginning. We will discuss this more, further along in the book. Once you understand as much as possible about your target market and your business, then you will be in a position to go searching for your ideal location.

My long time business associate and friend, Gerry Lazar, has a knack for finding small chains and helping them double, triple, or quadruple in a fairly short period of time. He looks for businesses that already have some momentum, a clear direction, and a well thought out business concept and brand. He has done this with independent fashion store chains, franchised chains, and specialty grocery store chains, to name a few. When you are ready and in motion, we can help you move into growth at warp speed. Our retail site selection company is called Top Cats Realty Inc. It is a commercial real estate brokerage with the single focus of growing retail, service, restaurant, and grocery chains. To find out more about how Top Cats can help your business grow, visit us at www.topcats.ca.

Finally, throughout this book, I make references to Blockbuster Video. Blockbuster Video's locations were top notch. I was part of their real estate team when they opened their first 350 stores in Canada in record time. Their site selection criteria were strictly adhered to, or we did not get approval to proceed with the deal. Many of the secrets known by the large, very successful, national restaurant and retail chains will be revealed as you read, chapter by chapter, through this book.

"Location, location, location," is an old, overused cliché, and few people really know what it means. So, read and learn; then, do what this book teaches, and your business will be well on the road to success.

Some of the names of people and companies in this book are real and others are fictitious for privacy purposes.

The Book on Retail Site Selection

To learn more and to sign up for our on-line training program, visit www.thedragonbooks.com.

[1] Small Business and the Economy. Small Business & Entrepreneurship Council. Web. 07 Feb. 2017.

[2] Key Small Business Statistics - August 2013 How many jobs do small businesses create?" Innovation, Science and Economic Development Canada, Government of Canada, 03 Mar. 2013.

Chapter 1

Why Do You Need a Bricks and Mortar Location for Your Business in the Age of E-commerce?

If you can operate from your basement or garage, why not do it and get the tax write off?

Quiz question: Can you name a company that is successful today, and was started in a garage? If you answered Apple, Microsoft, Google, HP, Amazon, or Mattel, just to name a few, you win. Starting off in a garage or basement is a great way to save money while getting your venture off the ground. That is, if you don't get shut down or fined for a zoning by-law infraction or fall victim to complaints from the neighbors.

The nature of your business or use as it is known in the world of site selection, is what dictates the location of the business. A high tech start up can be spawned in a garage or a basement, and can then be moved to an office environment when the time is right. However, if you are a retailer, service provider, or restaurateur, your business will need a location where you can serve your customers in person, right from the outset.

Looks Familiar?

To see a full color version of this cartoon go to
www.thedragonbooks.com

The Touch Factor – You can't get a haircut on the Internet

Nor can you get a massage, get your teeth cleaned, or have a romantic dinner with your sweetheart. The Internet is massively changing how we shop, how we entertain ourselves, and how we do our regular errands. And we've only seen the tip of the iceberg. Have you noticed the downsizing or disappearance of some of your favorite retail stores? At one time there were lots of cool and unique specialty bookstores and music shops that have all but disappeared. Shopping for books and music were two of the first retail experiences that were forever changed by the web. Next on the chopping block may be your favorite department store.

The point is, no matter how much e-commerce replaces the need for retail stores, there will always be some uses that require a building. Services of all sorts, entertainment venues, specialty grocery stores, and destination restaurants, are being targeted by high productivity shopping centers like never before. Gyms and specialized fitness like spin cycle and aerial yoga are exotic uses that have fitness conscious customers coming back to the malls regularly. Some service uses are no longer being relegated only to the less desirable *service corridors*, which normally means lower traffic than the main runs in a shopping center.

Last week, I was in the middle of printing one of those sixty-page retail lease documents when my printer ran out of ink. I needed two copies of the document for a meeting the same day. So, I zoomed over to the business supply store, hoping and praying they would have the right ink cartridge for my printer. They did; thanks Staples! I then thought to myself, there will continue to be a need for bricks and mortar retail stores like Staples, for just such instances. I did not have the time to order the ink cartridge on line. Same day delivery may become a reality soon, but it's not here yet. They may not need as much square footage as they

Español

have now, but I certainly appreciate knowing their retail store will be there to cover my next business emergency.

Destination versus Impulse – Is your business a destination? Would your customers seek you out even if you located your retail business in some obscure industrial park or at the end of a long corridor? Or, does your business depend on impulse purchases where you rely on lots of customer traffic to just happen upon your store, trip through the door, and buy something. If the purchase was unplanned and not premeditated, chances are, you have an impulse store. If you find something to carry that is truly unique and the word gets out, you may be able to re-create your store as a destination.

The reason you need to know if your business is a destination or an impulse store is crucial, because it will influence your location search. I know of a specialty knitting and weaving shop that carries hard-to-get yarn from Peruvian Alpacas and natural fibres that include blends of wool, silk, and cotton from Germany and Italy. Knitters, spinners, and weaving enthusiasts come from miles around to visit this shop because of its unique product offering. As the owner of a destination, you need only provide a location that ideally has free parking and is not too hard to find. You may choose to locate where you can pay cheaper rent or buy your own building on the edge of town and have little concern for what other uses are around you. You may wish to be on a transit route for employees or customers that do not drive. Lynn, the owner of Threads in Time, told me that one of the most popular services she offers are her specialty knitting classes. I thought they would attract only local knitting enthusiasts, but she said she quite often has students that travel hundreds of miles to attend her classes.

Store front photo, Threads in Time

To see a full color photograph, please visit
www.thedragonbooks.com

Yarn , Threads in Time

To see a full color photograph, please visit
www.thedragonbooks.com

If you are the owner of a destination retail store, and the local mall comes to invite you to become one of their tenants, remember, you attract customer traffic that they want; so, in negotiating your lease, ask for the world, and you may well get it.

Another great example of destination retail is George's Trains. George's is an extraordinary example of a destination retailer that sells model trains and accessories to customers literally from all over the world. George's Trains has been in business since 1962.

The current location is in a semi-industrial building, off the beaten path, next to the train tracks, which in this case is a cool thing. George's Trains is located right alongside a level train track crossing. So, while you are visiting the store, there is a good chance you will see the train crossing the road, with the gates in action, the lights flashing, and the bells ringing—a thrilling event to a model train enthusiast. It's all about the *experience*, the owner told me. I thought that most of their sales would come from their e-commerce site, but George's customers travel from far and wide to come to the store for the experience. As soon as you enter, you will see a full model train set up, complete with bridges and water, mountains and tunnels, and, of course, the model train including a great variety of train cars. The store is filled with all things model trains and even boasts a set of bleachers by the windows so customers can sit and watch the full size trains coming and going just outside the store.

George's Trains storefront

To see the full color photograph, please visit
www.thedragonbooks.com

Level Train Crossing near George's Trains

To see a full color photograph, please visit
www.thedragonbooks.com

Branding – without it, you're Chopped Liver, and you won't get the site you want

Imagine that you are the landlord of a retail property, and your best corner, with fabulous exposure and a great little patio, is now vacant and available for lease. You have decided you want to lease it to a coffee shop. So, if you had the choice, would you choose Joe's Café, or would you choose Starbucks? Some might say Joes Café, but with Starbucks you know what you are going to get. You know the menu, store design, how they operate, and you will love what the strength of Starbuck's brand will do for the value of your real estate. You also know that you will likely have them there for the next 10 years or more and that you will get your rent check on the first of the month, every month. That's the power of a brand.

I have been leasing retail properties for many years; it never fails to amaze me how consistently people call me to lease a space I have available, and they have no business plan, no brand, and no idea what they want to do. Which brings me to a story I would like to share with you— the story of Shinaz and Amad.

I had a retail space for lease, a former restaurant on the main street with good access and egress, exposure, signage, traffic galore, lots of free parking, and a nice little patio. A lovely young couple had their residential agent call me to book an appointment to tour the space. I am calling them Shinaz and Amad (not their real names). They wanted to open a pizza and shawarma restaurant. Since they weren't a branded restaurant, I knew the landlord would want to see a detailed business plan including menu, prices, store design, graphics and, especially, financial reports. Not only would he want to see sales projections but also how much money they had to start with, how much working capital they had, and how much they were planning to invest in the renovation. There had previously been a branded burger franchise there, and it had only lasted for one 5-year term.

The conversation between the residential agent and myself went something like this:

Tom (the residential agent): "I don't really have much experience in commercial, can you help me? I have these clients that want to open a restaurant in your space."

Me: "Where can I see the restaurant that your clients have now?"

Tom: "Well, this will actually be their first business."

Me: "Great, may I see their business plan? It will need to be detailed since it is all I will have to sell the landlord on their concept."

Tom: "Well, they don't have a business plan".

Me: "How about the menu? Do they have that figured out?"

Tom: "Aaaaa...why don't I let my clients tell you about it?"

(End of conversation)

Can you see the pattern here? It just so happened that the landlord had asked to be present for the meeting, and this couple and their inexperienced agent were completely unprepared. We've all heard the saying, "You get one chance to make a good first impression." Amad had worked in his family's restaurant in another city, so he had some restaurant experience. Shinaz had worked in the marketing department for a large retail chain. The landlord was willing to give them a chance and allowed them to have their agent submit an Offer to Lease, without a business plan. Upon reviewing the offer, the landlord made the deal conditional on the couple hiring a professional restaurant designer to help them create their concept and the renderings of how the restaurant would look upon completion. The hiring of a professional designer would have been an investment of about $3,000.00, and the couple refused to spend it. So, the deal died. I was surprised that they even got that far.

This sad drama is all too common. Can you pick out what mistakes caused this deal to die? Shinaz and Amad's first mistake was their failure to plan. If they had created a *brand*, worked on the menu, graphics, colors, interior look, and prototype design, and if they had documented their research of the competitive environment and target market, they may have had a chance of impressing the landlord and setting themselves up for success. Another less obvious but serious mistake they made was choosing to use their residential real estate agent. If they had hired an experienced commercial agent specializing in retail, they would have increased their chances of successfully leasing that location.

Synergy with neighboring businesses (also known as "co-tenancies")

Have you ever noticed that there are multiple shoe retailers in your favorite mall? If you were the owner of one of those shoe stores, would it not make more sense to be the only shoe retailer in the whole mall and have no competition? Savvy landlords know that by having multiple branded shoe stores, for example, in their retail mix, they will attract more shoppers. And, ultimately, all the various footwear retailers, and the whole mall for that matter, will benefit by having lots of shoppers.

When I worked as a real estate manager for Blockbuster Video, their preference was to be in a visible, freestanding building at the front of a busy grocery anchored plaza with a lot of *generators*.

What are generators, you ask? Let's say your business is a hair salon. Generators are the types of retail uses that generate daily traffic to the plaza; for example, a grocery store, a pharmacy or drug store, banks and credit unions, liquor and beer store, post office, driver's license bureau, some restaurants, etc. The more errands your customer can complete while she is in the vicinity of your salon, the greater are the chances of her coming to your salon more often. So, between her usual cut and color, because you are so conveniently located, she may drop in to buy from you her salon quality shampoo and her favorite nail polish.

Creating confidence within your target market – here today and…still here tomorrow

Having a bricks and mortar location for your business creates confidence in your customer base. Recently, my husband decided to buy a well-known branded language-learning course. He found it available from two large retail chains for basically the same price. Then he found it on a popular buy and sell website for less. He decided to buy it for less, met with the individual that was selling it, paid cash, and brought it home. Upon loading it on his computer, he realized the activation code would not work. He contacted the vendor, and guess what? He was nowhere to be found. My husband then called the manufacturer and they said they could not help him. If he had purchased it from one of the retail chains, he would simply have brought it back for a full refund or a new copy that works. He feels embarrassed about the whole thing, so please don't tell him I told you this story. The point is, a physical location for your business goes a long way to creating a lasting relationship between you and your customer base.

If you are paying attention to trends in the retail industry, you will know that e-commerce giants like Amazon are growing in leaps and bounds, and many bricks and mortar retailers are floundering. This trend will continue, and shifts are happening due to changes in consumer shopping habits.

But this is not the end of bricks and mortar stores—far from it—just like the advent of television did not bring about the end of radio, like some had predicted. Email was thought to be the death of postal mail, but that has not happened yet. New technologies seem to dovetail with existing technology and will continue to do so. Some industries seem to hang on to older technologies longer for some reason. At the time of this writing, the fax machine is still used by physicians and pharmacies to confirm patients' prescriptions, and some residential real estate offices and law offices still communicate via fax.

The bricks and mortar retail store that steps up its customer experience will not only flourish but will outpace e-commerce only retailers. Proximity marketing is now becoming popular. When a customer has a particular store's app on their mobile device, and is walking near that store, the customer will receive an automated incentive message (a coupon or promotional offer) to try and draw her into the store.

There will be an increase in the use of technology by bricks and mortar retailers to improve not only the customer's in-store experience but also software to merge data to improve logistics, operations, and even better predictions on upcoming fashion trends, designs, and colors.

The Real Cost of buying your own building to house your business location

If your dream is to build a successful retail, service, or restaurant business, then I suggest that you lease your premises. The reason for this is because things change! The location that you chose for your business may have made sense five or 10 years ago, but now your business will have evolved and the plaza or place will have changed. The changes may be good or bad, but you will need to evaluate their effect on your business and where you want to go with it in the next 5 to 10 years.

You need to start the evaluation process a full year prior to your notice of renewal date. If, upon the completion of your evaluation, you have decided that you will need to relocate, you will require up to 12 months to find your new ideal location, negotiate your agreement to lease, and build out your leasehold improvements. You may need even more than 12 months to make all of that happen in time, in order to open when you close your existing location.

If you make the decision to buy a building to house your business, you may find that the success of your retail business will be compromised because your building is no longer its ideal location. The process of selling your building can take a very long time and can ultimately be detrimental to the profitability of your business.

If you are compelled to invest in commercial real estate, then you should proceed to create a real estate investment company. That is a very different business from running a store or restaurant.

Kelly C. Laughton

Why buying a retail condominium for your business is almost always a bad idea

A question I often get asked is "Should I invest in a retail condominium for my business?" My answer so far has always been no. And here's why: in almost every retail condominium complex I have seen, investors who have purchased the condos want the maximum possible rent for their premises and have no regard for the retail mix of the complex. That means that there is no common landlord controlling the uses. With no exclusive rights over your use, the retail condo next door to you can be the same business use as yours. So, if you open Mimi's Nail Salon, there is nothing stopping Millie's Nail Salon from moving in next door. You may also end up near uses that you don't like; for example, a marijuana shop, a tattoo parlor, or a smelly soap store.

Retail Condominiums-two competing nail salons beside each other

Sale/Lease Back & Right of First Refusal

If you own the building that houses your business and you do not want to move yet, you may be able to find a buyer for your building and remain there as a tenant. This is called a sale/lease back. The reason you may wish to do this is because you have plans to open a second location elsewhere, and you want to use the capital from your building to open your new location. There could be many reasons why you would do this. Regardless, it will provide you with greater flexibility for making a move in the future.

If you are still motivated by the real estate investment opportunity where you are opening your business, you may, as part of your lease agreement, be able to negotiate a right of first refusal to buy the plaza or property from your landlord, if and when it becomes available for sale.

Settling for the wrong location for cheaper rent or other concessions

Imagine making a decision to put your business in a rundown property that is slated for demolition, because the rent is cheaper than all the other vacancies in the area.

What do you think you are communicating to your customers, clients or patients? I know from personal experience that I judge the cleanliness of a restaurant's kitchen by the cleanliness of its washrooms. The same goes for any food or health care related uses.

You may think that you got a great deal, but if you have learned anything from this book so far, the rent is only one of the pieces of the puzzle.

When I pull into a plaza where the parking lot is strewn with garbage and full of potholes, the sidewalk is broken, the glass is cracked, and the garbage cans are over flowing, I immediately wonder if the property is slated for demolition. Whether or not that is the case, it makes me suspect that the retailers in that plaza won't be there much longer. It also tells me as a consumer that I don't want to do business with the tenants in this plaza because, if they don't care about their location, they won't care about me as their customer.

Retailing from industrial space is sometimes done effectively. I remember a fun fashion store that had some great lines and appealing prices, if you were willing to make the drive. It was a store in an industrial building on the edge of town in a suburb. They advertised like mad on radio and newspaper, and had giant signs. The building was painted in bright yellow and was surrounded by big, fake palm trees. It was hard to miss. It was quite a success for more than two decades. The money they saved on rent went into advertising. After the arrival of the world-wide-web, advertising became much less effective and, soon, the business closed.

The point is, there are many options that could work for your business. So, if you are willing to pay higher rents for a purportedly high traffic location, do your due diligence. Go there morning, noon, and night. Count the cars, count the pedestrians, and count the number of shoppers with bags versus those without. Talk to the other retailers. Find out how they are doing and how long they have been there. Caveat emptor—let the buyer beware.

Now that you know about rent, zoom to the next chapter to learn how to promote your location and really take advantage of your carefully selected bricks and mortar.

Chapter 2

The Five "Ps" of Marketing and How they Affect Your Choice of Location: People, Product, Price, Promotion, and Place

This book is about choosing the right *place* for the success of your business. The other 4 "P"s of marketing will drive the creation of your site selection criteria.

Have you ever looked at the annual report for a company? Either on the front cover or close to the front of the report, they will proudly feature a photograph of their head office—their "real estate." They may not even own that real estate; it could simply be leased space. So, why are they so proud of it? Because their choice of physical location makes a statement about the company and their brand. An impressive looking head office shows stability, strength, longevity, and credibility, to name just a few attributes.

Why do you think Tiffany's, Ralph Lauren and Saks pay some of the highest rents in the world to have a location on Manhattan's Fifth Avenue? It's all about maintaining their image and brand in the minds and, especially, the pocket books of their target market.

People – Defining your Target Market and their wants, needs and desires

When I started as a shopping center marketing director back in the early 80s, I had some independent retailers in my shopping center, as well as some local merchants who had bought franchises. When I asked each of them the question, "Who is your target market?" the answer I commonly got was, "Oh, it's everybody." Typically, those were the retailers that were the lowest performers in the mall. So, on this topic, please take note: if you think your business appeals to everybody, it will likely appeal to nobody. It's like those pantyhose that are labeled "one size fits all." If you ever tried a pair on, you quickly learned, "one size fits no one." The more you can learn about your target market, the more you can appeal to their wants, needs, and desires. If you get really good at doing that, they'll keep coming back, over and over again, and they'll even bring their friends and family. Identify the emotional connection between your real business and your customers' desires, and you'll have found your key to success.

Demographics and Psychographics

So, what are demographics and psychographics, and what are they good for? Your target market can be defined based on where they live in relation to your location, as well as gender, age group, income level, or education level.

Psychographics is the science of grouping people that have similar attitudes, values, or lifestyles. Knowing this information before you choose your location could save you from disaster.

The story I am about to tell you will help to demonstrate this point. The group I'm referring to is a team of Chinese grocery store operators who are mostly Mandarin speaking immigrants from Mainland China. They found and leased a vacant grocery store in a busy area that had previously been operated by one of the national grocery chains. The national chain had moved up the street to a larger and more visible site. This Chinese business team was a group of experienced grocers and knew how to run a supermarket. They called it Jackson's Fresh Foods (after President Andrew Jackson who is on the US twenty dollar bill). They worked hard to renovate the store and filled it up with all the products they normally sold. The grand opening day came and, despite all the advertising they did, very few customers showed up. This miniscule stream of shoppers continued for weeks to the point where, if something did not change, they would surely go bankrupt.

So, they started asking questions of their suppliers, other retailers, and their advertising sales representatives. They soon learned that there were almost no Chinese people living in that neighborhood. The dominant ethnic groups were East Europeans, including Polish, Ukrainian, Czech, and Russian. They quickly began to learn what food products and services appealed to those demographics. It was a big learning curve, but they were fast learners and it got them focused on studying area demographics before opening other new stores.

Where are they coming from and where are they headed?

Knowing where your customers are headed, before and after they patronize your location, can be the difference between success and failure for your business. Take for example: Canada's coffee and donut chain, Tim Horton's. Can you guess which side of the street they want to be on? If you guessed "the going to work side," you win the Tim Bit. Although it seems that Tim's are now so successful, they will locate almost anywhere—the going to work side, the coming home side, the "let's go to Tim's drive thru and grab lunch" side, etc.

Proximity to Anchor Store

In general, a dollar store needs to be as close as possible to the entrance of the grocery store. Imagine a mother with a toddler and an infant. Once she has shopped for groceries and loaded the groceries into her car, if she has to drive across the parking lot to the dollar store, guess what? She's not going. After completing the process of strapping her little ones into their car seats, she is not going to the dollar store. She's most likely headed for home.

Product or Service – What is your *real business*?

It's important to understand your real business. What do you think is the real business of McDonalds—hamburgers and fries? McDonalds is actually in the business of selling fun. Did you know that McDonalds is one of the world's top sellers of toys? No doubt those brightly colored play rooms with the cool slides are a kid magnet. And how about those Golden arches? Ever notice how they are perfectly positioned so that little passengers in car seats in the back can all scream together when they see them?

What if you own a Mercedes dealership; are you in the business of selling cars or are you promoting membership in an exclusive community that identifies with luxury, prestige, comfort, and the latest in automotive engineering?

Now, take a moment, sit back, close your eyes, and think about your *real business* or the business you would like to be in. Are you a dentist? Why do your patients come to you, year after year, instead of switching to the new dental office that just opened by their home or work? Is it because they trust you? Is there something that makes you different from your competitors? What is it? Try hard to understand why you clients come to you. If you don't know, ask them. Find a way to appeal to your customers on an emotional level.

Price – How will you know what rent your business can afford and how will it affect the price of your offering?

We have a client that is a franchisee of a national dollar store chain. We have been successful at acquiring some large, high traffic retail spaces at low rents for this retailer. In one case, the Landlord was willing to do a rent deal at a percentage of sales. In that center, the landlord took a gamble and won because the gross rent (net rent plus common area maintenance plus realty taxes) that would have been negotiated is actually lower than what the tenant is paying in rent as percentage of sales. That is because the tenant is doing very well and the sales are impressive. This is a particularly skilled retail team that has dozens of stores.

They do their own buying in the Far East and really understand their business.

The low rent or, in this case, rent that is a percentage of sales, allows this retailer to offer amazing deals to its shoppers. The store works on a large volume of transactions and the landlord's shopping center benefits by the strong traffic that the store generates. *If you are new at retail, please don't expect to start at this level.

On the topic of rent, one of the most important things to know about your business is how much it can afford to pay in rent and be profitable. This information comes from your business plan. In retail space (as in office and industrial space), the rent is calculated based on the square footage of your leased premises. Rent includes minimum rent (also called base rent or net rent) and common area maintenance (also called C.A.M., T.M.I., or additional rent). Added to that is your realty tax. The landlord gets a realty tax bill from the municipal government and then charges it back to the tenants based on *proportionate share*. So, your portion of the realty tax bill is the tax amount per square foot times your square footage.

Gross Occupancy Cost

Typical retail businesses' gross occupancy cost is anywhere from 5% to 12% of gross sales. It can be lower or higher than that range, and it is up to you to learn what that factor is for your particular business category. Then, you estimate your sales on a monthly basis. It is common to negotiate a rent that starts at a lower rate per square foot to allow for time to build sales volume. That is why rents will typically escalate over the term of the lease.

How will your rent (and location) ultimately affect your target market's perception of the prices you are charging for your products or services?

We have a specialty high-end giftware client that opened in a redeveloped shopping center anchored by Whole Foods in an upscale downtown neighborhood. The rent is quite high but is in line with the prices of the products they are selling. Their offering includes functional art pieces and handmade artisan creations in silver and stainless steel. These beautiful gift items come from

Denmark, Germany, Italy, and USA. If this store had been located in a "B" mall or next to the dollar store in a low rent plaza, they would not be successful. Their target market would not find them and, if they did, they would expect a deep discount from you. When you are charging thousands of dollars for a bowl, your location and co-tenants need to be in line with the demographics of your target market.

Promotion – 79% of the Buying Decision is made on-line prior to visiting the store

With the right location, more than half of your promotional job is done. As soon as I write this, this chapter will be out of date; in fact, a number of things in this book will be, given how fast technology is now changing. As of now there are *on-line only* retailers that do not have a bricks and mortar presence, and there are bricks and mortar retailers that do not have an on-line presence. We are currently seeing the importance of having both working together to create what is called omni-channel retailing. This topic will be dealt with in greater detail in Chapter 9.

Most of the traditional methods of paid advertising have all but disappeared. Social Media marketing is no longer optional. If you do not yet have an on-line presence, you are going to need one. Your web site must be easy to find and navigate. You will also ideally invest in an app that will allow customers to find you on their mobile devices and quickly access your address, hours of operation, offerings, and prices.

The branding part of your business is more critical now than ever. I recommend that you read the book called **Branding Small Business for Dummies** by NY Times Top Ten Best Selling Author Raymond Aaron. For your free e-book, go to www.thedragonbooks.com

Now, zoom along to Chapter 3 where you will learn how not to lose your shirt (or worse) by picking the wrong location.

Chapter 3

"PLACE," the Most Crucial "P," and the Focus of This Book.

"Pretend that the business you own—or want to own—is the prototype, or will be the prototype for 5,000 more just like it."
Michael E. Gerber the E-Myth Revisited

Choose the wrong location and you could lose your shirt, or worse...

The reason I'm saying that "place" is the most dangerous "P" is not to scare you so much as to warn you of the commitments you are making when you sign your binding offer to lease. The reason why the retail lease is such a long and detailed document (often 60 or more legal size pages), is because it is governing the relationship between your business and your landlord for the next 5 or 10 years, or more. An agreement of purchase and sale is, by contrast, a relatively short document, because once a property is bought by the buyer and sold by the seller, that is pretty much the end of the relationship.

The business owner that signs the lease without reviewing it, or hiring an experienced retail lease lawyer to negotiate it on his behalf, is in line for a rude awakening, if and when a problem arises. There will be more on retail lease lawyers later.

Have you ever noticed that the biggest expense on most income statements is *rent*?

This is one of the most important reasons to get it right when choosing your business location. Your rent and *occupancy costs* will likely be the largest expense on your income statement. Rent is a fixed expense, payable whether you make $1.00 or $10,000.00. In addition to your base rent or net rent (in North America it is quoted on a per square foot basis), you will pay your proportionate share of realty taxes and common area charges. In a retail unit, you will normally have meters to measure your usage of utilities such as electricity, natural gas, and water. And, in most cases, you will pay those monthly charges directly to the utility company.

Percentage Rent

If you decide to lease space in an enclosed shopping center, you will encounter a term in your lease called percentage rent. The concept here is that if your sales are really high and they exceed a pre-negotiated sales threshold, then you will be obligated to pay an additional amount of rent to the landlord. Most retailers don't mind paying percentage rent because they are usually doing really well in order to exceed their natural percentage rent sales threshold. It's a good problem to have.

Your business plan and why it drives your entire site selection process

Business Plan: two dirty little words that so many new business people don't even want to utter. I get countless phone calls on my listed retail spaces from people that don't seem to have spent even 5 minutes on their proposed business before they go looking for a space for lease. Is it possible that a new entrepreneur, while sitting at home, gets the idea to open up a business and immediately jumps in his car and goes driving around in search of "FOR LEASE" signs? I know that sounds crazy, but that's how it seems.

They're excited to actually get a live person to talk to on the phone. They ask endless questions like how big, how much, and when? I say, "I'm happy to provide you with all those details, but I have some restrictive covenants; may I please know what use you are proposing?" In other words, "What do you want to do?" Amazingly, that question is often a stumper. Now, I'm not suggesting that everyone is like this, but it is astounding how often this occurs. Maybe that's one of the reasons why there is such a high failure rate with new businesses?

By contrast, I recently had the privilege of doing two Domino's Pizza deals with an experienced franchisee team, a father and son that own about 15 locations. They were real professionals. They knew everything about their business, and I mean everything. When I sat down to work out the terms of the deal, they knew the answer to almost every question I asked. It didn't take us long to figure out what would work for them and what would work for my client, the landlord.

Your business plan does not have to be an epic saga. Here are some basic topics to cover:

1. Define the problem you're going to solve. This should answer the question of "why" start the business in the first place.
2. Explain how your product or service will solve the problem defined in #1. This should answer the question of "what" you are going to do.
3. Describe the people that have this problem and their common characteristics. This is the answer to the question, "Who?"
4. Describe the current state of your market, competition, and industry; this is where you get to show off with colorful charts and graphs. This should include the answer to the question, "When?"
5. Explain how you will make money. This is your "How."
6. This is a critical piece for anyone trying to land a great location for their business. Invest in a prototype design: a colorful artist's rendering of how your business will look. Do a floor plan, a storefront elevation, and a materials sample board. Add some great shots of your product line or the services you plan to offer. If it is a restaurant, include the mock-up of your menu. In all cases, ensure your trade name and graphics are dynamite—a real home run.

This will go a long way to impressing a landlord and helping you get the best possible location and deal.

Artist's Rendering-Taquito, a quick service food-court concept courtesy Michael Gouveia, Creative Director Unparallel Brand +Design

See the full color prototype store design and materials sample board at www.thedragonbooks.com.

Defining your Site Selection Criteria

For almost any type of retail store, service business, or restaurant, you will want the best exposure and visibility. Remember the old saying, "Out of sight, out of mind." It may sound like a cliché, but it's true. Otherwise, if you can operate out of your basement or garage, why not do it? Unless you have a destination use as previously described, pay close attention to this advice. The needs of your target market must be in your frontal cortex while creating your SSC (site selection criteria). If you are opening a physiotherapy clinic, you will want to ensure that there are no barriers to your entrance; likewise, if you are selling mobility products to seniors or people of any age who have special needs. If your target market is a mother with babies and toddlers, ensure that she can get into the store and move around easily with her baby carriage or stroller. Also, ensure that the washrooms are fitted with changing tables and a rest area for breast-feeding. And don't forget about the fathers. In many cases, these days, the dads are the primary caregivers for the children.

The WOW Factor – How to get the Landlord to "want" you and why that's so important

By doing a really great job of your business plan, your artist's rendering of your prototype design (if it is a new concept), and material sample board, you will get a lot of "WOWS" whenever you present your concept. When you show it to the bank that you are trying to borrow money from, do you think your chances will be improved when you get a lot of WOWS? How about when you show the landlord that owns the location you really want to lease. When the landlord gets excited because he can see the potential in your fabulous concept and business plan, suddenly he wants to attract you and your business. You may find that the rent numbers get more flexible, the tenant improvement allowance becomes more generous, or the best space—end cap space—is offered when you didn't even think it was available.

Now, zoom to the next chapter to learn the six most important steps on how to choose the right location for your business.

Chapter 4

The Six Steps on How to Choose the Right Location for YOUR Business (the meat and potatoes of site selection)

Your Site selection criteria, as defined in Chapter 3

In Chapter 3, we talked about how to define your target market, understanding your "real business," and you learned the importance of understanding your customers' wants, needs, and desires. Based on that information, you are now ready to choose three possible locations that qualify to meet your site selection criteria.

Trade area, competition, and demographics

If you are already in business, you can get a pretty good picture of your current trade area just by collecting customer zip or postal codes and plotting them on a postal walk map. There are lots of analytics companies that will do this for you for a fee, but you can do this simple exercise yourself for free. This will show you from where and how far your customers are willing to travel. If it is a new business, use Google Earth to establish a trade area based on a typical drive time for your particular business or industry average. Use one of your three target sites.

A hair salon, for example, may estimate its trade area to be a 10-minute drive radius. Here is where I suggest you get into your car and literally drive for 10 minutes in all four directions from the subject site. Take a paper map with you and let X mark your subject site. So, that means starting at the site and driving for 10 minutes north (mark that point on the map), and then driving back to your starting point. Now drive 10 minutes to the south (and again mark the 10 minute point on the map), and so on until you have driven for 10 minutes in all four directions. During this exercise, observe what you see. Take note of the rooftops; are they apartment buildings or single-family dwellings? Are there elementary schools, high schools, office towers, or industrial parks? Take note of the speed limit on the road and drive at that speed. Think of the demographics you ordered for that 10-minute radius to see if they match what you are observing. Some areas change quite quickly and, typically, census data are two to four years out of date.

You may feel that observing the trade area via Google Maps or some other on-line service is adequate, but there is no replacement for what you will learn by personally making the drive. I have observed, that before the final sign-off happens, by even the largest retail chains, the CEO or other C level officer of the company will personally visit the site.

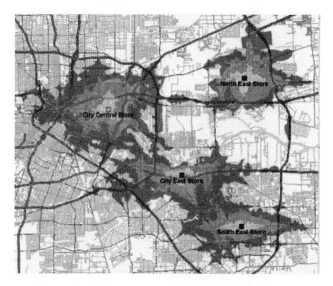

Trade Areas of a four-store network,
showing 3, 6 and 9-minute drive times

To see the full color version of this map, go to
www.thedragonbooks.com

The next step is to plot the competition within that trade area. Then, estimate the total hair salon dollars being spent by your target market in your proposed trade area. You can get statistics from the consumer expenditure reports from the same source as the demographic reports. Now, plot your competitors on the map. Visit your competitors and learn as much as you can about them, without getting arrested. That exercise will help establish the size of the pie in hair salon dollars per year and how much of a slice you expect to get.

This is a 3-mile radius ring showing the subject site at the center

To see the full color map please go to
www.thedragonbooks.com

Visibility/exposure, access/egress, parking, barrier free access

No matter what business you are in, it's hard to argue against the value of great exposure. That's why you see the strongest brands in the buildings that are set closest to the street and often have the drive-thrus. They are called pad buildings or out parcels. The financial institutions, McDonalds, Starbucks, and the large pharmacy chains get locations with the best exposure. They also pay higher rents and commonly must provide the landlord with significant financial security in order to get them. But those chains know that the extra expenses for the higher profile locations will be justified in higher sales.

To evaluate the access and egress of a site, you need to drive to the proposed location and go through the exercise of entering and exiting from every point. Do this exercise at different times of the day and different days of the week. If you can enter ok, but you can't easily exit, from say 4:00 until 6:00 pm some weekdays, it could be a problem. It may be ok for some retailers whose customers visit less frequently, but it may not work for your business. You also need to be aware of the parking lot and where shoppers are currently parking. Also, beware of parking hog uses like gyms, bowling alleys, many entertainment venues, buffet restaurants, etc. You may say to yourself, "Great, look at all the traffic." But take a closer look and you will learn that the gym members come to your site; some will park in front of your store for 2 hours, then leave and go straight home. Meanwhile, your customers will have to park further away from your store and may not be happy about it.

On the topic of accessibility, you will want to ensure there is easy wheel chair access, ramps instead of curbs, a wheelchair accessible washroom, and handicap parking near your entrance.

Traffic – vehicular and pedestrian, daytime versus nighttime

When my husband and I were visiting London, England, we found a quick service restaurant called Pret A Manger (French for "Ready to Eat"). Their site selection was wonderful. Every time we arrived in a different area of London via the Tube, it seemed like Pret A Manger was right there. The locations they chose had high visibility, throngs of pedestrian traffic, and excellent signage. They were not near any parking; their customers were all on foot. Their food offering was fresh, ready to eat sandwiches and soups, and a great selection of snacks that always seemed to be the right size and price. They also have great baristas that make a fabulous latte and really good hot chocolate. As of this writing, there are 296 Pret A Manger shops in the UK alone, and they are also in USA, China, Hong Kong, France, and Dubai.

Do you think they did some pedestrian traffic counts before deciding where to locate? I would also suspect they know quite a lot about their target market (tourists), where we were coming from (the subway station) and where we were headed (Piccadilly Circus). They also seemed to know we were hungry, time tapped, and wanting to grab n go.

The daytime traffic versus nighttime traffic of your subject site is another topic for you to research. There is an underground pathway system in the downtown of Toronto, Canada that covers 18 miles or 30 km. It is known simply as *the Path*. The pedestrian traffic down there from 7:00am to 6:00pm, Monday through Friday, is amazing. The 1,200 shops and services located in the Path do very well during those hours. The traffic during evenings and weekends is, by contrast, quite low. Your business plan should include your hours of operation and will thereby guide you in this important site selection decision.

End cap versus in-line and distance from the "Generators"

In your site research process, take note of which retail tenants have the best and most visible locations. If there is a pad with a drive thru, is it a bank or one of the national fast foods chains like McDonalds, Wendy's, or A&W? If there is no pad building opportunity, you will likely find the national brand on the end cap. The reason for this is that they will not accept anything less. These brands have clearly defined their site selection criteria, and they stick to it. There may be an exception to the rule where the desired real estate does not exist at the geographical co-ordinates they have targeted.

Assuming you want the most visible spot in the development, if you can secure the best end cap, closest to the generators like the grocery store, the bank or the pharmacy, then do it. You can usually expect to pay a higher rate/square foot than an in-line space or a space that has compromised visibility or parking.

End Cap-Retail Plaza, courtesy Lisgar Development

Aerial photograph of the above retail plaza
Example of free standing buildings, end caps, and in-line units,
courtesy Lisgar Development

To see a full color photograph, please visit
www.thedragonbooks.com

Signage

As a former real estate manager for Blockbuster Video, we generally negotiated the signage clause first. If we could not secure the "torn ticket logo" on a freestanding pole sign or on the top of the landlord's shared pylon sign, in many cases we would move along to the next deal. Even if the site was close to ideal in other ways, we knew the real estate committee at head office would not approve it without that torn ticket logo in full view. That's how important signage was to Blockbuster.

It is just as important for the success of your business. If you are considering locating in an outdoor retail center with many other retailers, there may be a waiting list to get your sign on the pylon. Be persistent. Negotiate the right of first refusal in your lease to get on the pylon sign when the opportunity arises. And yes, there will be monthly rent to pay in order to be on the pylon. Pay it for the increased exposure it will provide—24/7.

Ensure you take advantage of every signage opportunity that your location offers. Signage is always subject to landlord approval and municipal approval. So, be proactive by having your sign designer create beautiful artist's renderings, showing how your fabulous graphics and colors with look above your store front, on the shared pylon sign, and anywhere else you can put your sign. Make these renderings part of your business plan. They are an important part of your WOW factor.

Have you ever noticed those entrance and exit signs that McDonalds uses to show you where to enter and how to get to their drive thru? They are an extra expense for the franchisee, so why do you think they do it?

Once you have completed your research and you have decided on your #1 top choice site, now is the time to connect with the landlord and generate your Offer to Lease.

Blockbuster's torn ticket

To see a full color version of this photograph, see
www.thedragonbooks.com

Now zip to Chapter 5 where you will learn how to get control of
your ideal site before someone else does.

Chapter 5

Locking it down!

The Letter of Intent or Offer to Lease

By creating your own Letter of Intent, you are able to put forward terms and issues that are important to your business right at the outset. The Letter of Intent (LOI for short) is a non-binding list of terms used to begin the discussion between a landlord and tenant. It is one way to test the water to see if the parties to the agreement are even in the same ball park before spending time and money on a detailed binding offer to lease.

The LOI outlines the following:

- Date
- Landlord Company, Tenant Company, and Tenant's Trade Name
- Address of subject property, unit number, square footage
- Minimum rent and additional rent
- Tenant Improvement Allowance, rent free period and Fixturing Period
- Term of lease and options to renew or extend
- Proposed commencement dates and any blackout periods (see glossary of terms)

- Financial Strength or covenant and/or guarantor of lease
- Use and Exclusive
- Conditions
- Landlord's Work and Tenant's Work
- Lease
- Signage
- Confidentiality
- Brokerage Commissions
- Disclaimers

The tenant or the tenant's mandated commercial real estate broker can generate the LOI. Once it has been created and tenant approved, it is then presented to the landlord or the landlord's leasing representative. Because it is a non-binding document, the response may not be formal. It may be verbal or a simple email. The landlord's response will give the tenant an indication of whether there is any need to go further. If the terms of each party are too far apart, there is no need to continue the discussion and both parties can move along. If, however, the tenant's terms are within a range that the landlord can accept, then it is worthwhile to get any changes in writing.

At this point, the landlord may take the initiative to incorporate the tenant's terms into its binding agreement to lease or full lease document. Once the agreement to lease has been generated by the landlord, and presented to the tenant, the tenant must then read it and will ideally forward a copy to the lawyer for the tenant. THIS IS A BINDING DOCUMENT! Just because it precedes the lease does not mean you are not obligated to fulfill its terms.

Some landlords proceed straight to the full lease document. If there has been a letter of intent or a term sheet used, the items that have been agreed upon by both parties should be incorporated in the lease.

Lawyers, Leases, and Lease Negotiations

I cannot emphasize enough the importance of working with an experienced lease lawyer that understands a retail lease document and how to protect the tenant in your relationship with the landlord. Most often, the lawyers that work for the landlord have written the lease document that gets signed. In other words the clauses in the lease are slanted in favor of the landlord.

In cases where my company was the listing brokerage and the tenant had its own agent, I was not allowed to provide advice to the tenant. The retail tenant must rely upon the advice of its representing agent. This is why it is also important to choose the right agent with retail leasing expertise, but there will be more on that topic later. I have at times witnessed the tenant choosing to bring her retail lease to the lawyer that she used when she bought her house. The result was a larger than necessary legal bill and a resulting lease that did not protect the tenant. A lawyer that is not familiar with a retail lease will need to spend time learning the meaning of some of the unique concepts he or she is not familiar with.

Meanwhile, a lawyer with deep lease expertise will immediately focus on the areas where he or she knows you will need protection or flexibility and will also be familiar with how far the landlord can be pushed when negotiating on behalf of the tenant.

Let's look at Joe and Christina who are new Yellow Submarine sandwich franchisees. The lease their landlord wants them to sign has a radius restriction of 4 miles. In other words, the landlord wants to stop Joe and Christina from opening another Yellow Submarine anywhere within a 4-mile radius of that landlord's site. Yellow Submarine's head office would not agree to that because they have every intention of opening more Yellow Submarines within the 4 mile radius of Joe and Christina's new site. The franchisor, in this case, Yellow Submarine, normally signs the lease corporately, then subleases or transfers the lease to the franchisees. The lawyer for the tenant needs to know what the radius agreement is between the franchisee and the franchisor. If it is 2 miles, then the lawyer for the tenant should explain this to the landlord's lawyer and the lease could then be changed to a radius restriction of 2 miles.

Your Use Clause and Restrictive Covenant

In a case where the tenant is a hair salon, the cutting, styling, and coloring of hair can be written up as the primary use. As ancillary to the *primary use*, the hair salon may wish to offer aesthetic services such as manicures and pedicures, hair removal, eyebrow and eye lash services, etc. In addition, the hair salon may also want the right to offer spa type services such as massage therapy, facials, and body wraps, at some point in the future. The landlord may agree to providing the hair salon exclusivity for cutting, styling, and coloring hair, the primary use, but may reserve the right to lease space in the plaza to a nail salon or a spa. So, what this means to the hair salon is that the landlord is agreeing to not allow any other competition in the plaza for cutting hair, but they are reserving the right to lease space to a nail salon or a spa, or both. If the landlord does not include the nail and spa services in the hair salon's use clause, the hair salon will be in contravention of its lease if they choose to do so. It may be possible to get those uses added to the tenant's use clause at a later date by way of a letter to the landlord and a subsequent Lease Amending Agreement signed by both parties.

If the tenant is an unbranded, independent hair salon with no other locations and little to offer in the way of financial strength, and the lawyer pushes too hard on behalf of the tenant for exclusivity on the other uses, the landlord may decide to abort the deal altogether. In a large retail property, the landlord would feel that it is a case of the tail wagging the dog.

This is when your lawyer's knowledge and experience can make all the difference. He or she may even have previously dealt with your landlord, and that in itself may provide an advantage.

**ARTICLE VI - USE OF THE LEASED PREMISES; PROMOTIONAL
AND ADVERTISING ACTIVITIES**

Section 6.01 - <u>Use of the Leased Premises</u>

The Tenant shall use the Leased Premises solely for the purpose of conducting the business of a hair salon, aesthetics, electrolysis and cosmetics and the Tenant will not use or permit, or suffer the use of the Leased Premises or any part thereof for any other business or purpose. In connection with the business to be conducted by the Tenant on the Leased Premises, the Tenant shall, prior to the Commencement Date advise the Landlord of its advertised name and shall thereafter use only such advertised name and will not change the advertised name of the business to be operated in the Leased Premises without the prior written consent of the Landlord.

This is an example of a use clause from an operating hair salon.

As a prospective retail tenant, your negotiating clout has everything to do with what you are bringing to the negotiating table. In a situation where the tenant is a 50,000 square foot specialty grocery store that will anchor the plaza, the use clause will include all the categories of foods and services to be sold by the grocery store. The exclusivity clause will include pretty much everything that is in the use clause. The landlord may request a "carve out" for the ability to be able to lease small stores in the plaza to a specialty bakery, for example, or a convenience store, not to be greater than say 3,000 square feet. The grocery store's exclusivity will likely extend to any adjacent lands owned by the landlord. As you can see in this example, the negotiating clout is with the anchor store.

EXCLUSIVE RIGHTS

The Lease shall provide that Tenant shall have the exclusive rights in the Development and on the Lands as they exist from time to time during the Term or any extension or renewal thereof, including any expansions of or additions to the Development or Lands and any abutting lands ("Abutting Lands") owned or controlled by the landlord or any affiliated party at any time during the Term (including any extension or renewal thereof), to the operation of a retail pharmacy and pharmaceutical dispensary and to the following purposes. Therefore, the Landlord covenants and agrees that it shall not lease, licence, suffer or permit the use of any other space in or on the Development, the Lands or Abutting Lands for the operation of a retail pharmacy or pharmaceutical dispensary or for any of the following purposes:

(i) for the sale of any items of merchandise requiring the approval or supervision of a registered or licensed pharmacist, save and except for the existing pharmacy in the ▓▓▓▓ premises under the terms of the ▓▓▓▓ lease;

(ii) for the operation of any store which sells general merchandise at one or more price points such as, by way of example, stores operating under the names ▓▓▓▓▓▓▓ Dollar", "Dollar ▓▓▓▓", "Dollar ▓▓▓▓" or "▓▓▓▓▓▓▓", save and except for the existing ▓▓▓▓▓▓▓ (its replacements, successors or assigns), comprising an area no greater than the existing premises of approximately 4,550 square feet;

(iii) for the operation of a convenience store, variety store or jug milk store, save and except for an existing convenience store (its replacements, successors or assigns) comprising an area no greater than the existing premises of approximately 1,600 square feet;

(iv) for the operation of a retail postal outlet;

(v) for the operation of a store whose principal business is the sale of health and beauty aids, save and except for the existing ▓▓▓▓▓▓▓ (its replacements, successors or assigns) comprising an area no greater than the existing premises of approximately 1,000 square feet;

(vi) for the operation of a store whose principal business is the sale of ▓▓▓▓ ▓▓▓▓

"Exclusive Rights" from an actual Lease

This *Exclusive Rights* clause is from an actual lease of an anchor store, and is an example of the lease protecting its in-store pharmacy, not only from any other pharmacies but also from a dollar store, a convenience store, a postal outlet, or any business whose principle use is that of health and beauty aids. So, when you call a retail leasing agent or leasing manager about a vacancy in a plaza you are interested in, they will want to know about your use. This is because there is a good chance there are use restrictive covenants in the complex that they must abide by.

Your terms and options to renew

It is generally to the tenant's advantage to choose a shorter lease term with options to renew. A five-year lease obligates the tenant to be responsible for 60 months of gross rent plus whatever other obligations there are in the lease. If the tenant chooses a ten-year term, there may be an advantage of negotiating a slightly better rental rate, but it also means that the tenant is now on the hook for 120 months of gross rent. Leases with franchisees are often 10 years because the franchise agreement (the agreement between the franchisee and the franchisor) is normally for 10 years.

When there is a five-year term with options to renew, the rents for one or two of the renewal periods can be pre-negotiated in the agreement. The problem with that, however, is that it is difficult to predict if market rents are going to be higher or lower, five or ten years into the future. Regardless, the option to renew is the tenant's right to renew or not to renew. So, that is why, as the tenant, you want to start negotiating your renewal a year or more prior to your renewal date. If you have an alternate location, or even two, where you know you could relocate if necessary, that puts you in a much stronger position if your landlord is playing tough with you on your renewal terms. There is more to know about how and when to negotiate your renewal but we will deal with those finer details in the *on-line Location Dragon, certification course.*

There is a date in the lease when the tenant is to provide notice to the landlord of its intention to renew or not to renew the lease. It is not the landlord's responsibility to remind you of that date.

Minimum (basic) rent, Common Area Maintenance (CAM), and Realty Taxes *See Bonus Chapter #10, by Retail Lease Expert Lawyer, Robert Kligerman

There are several terms for rent that mean pretty much the same thing. Basic rent, minimum rent, or net rent are the terms for the portion of what the tenant pays monthly to the landlord, usually on a per square foot basis. The net rent can be a different rate for each tenant, so don't bother comparing your rent to that of the business next door. The common area maintenance and the realty taxes are billed to the landlord, and then the landlord divides those bills by the gross leasable area of the property and charges them back on a per square foot basis to each of the tenants. Each tenant is then billed proportionally based on the square footage of each leased premises.

The expenses that make up the common area maintenance charges differ for every property but, typically, include landscaping/snow removal, parking lot sweeping, striping and repairs, utility charges for the parking lot, and any other common area lighting, security, garbage removal, pest control, superintendent's wages, and management fees. In an enclosed shopping center, this list is much longer and the charges are usually much higher. The realty tax bill is generally sent to the landlord, and that too is charged back to the tenants on a proportionate share basis.

In an enclosed shopping center, there is a concept known as *percentage rent*, which means the landlord gets rewarded for helping you do really well. Please see the glossary for the definition of percentage rent.

The Roof and HVAC units are two lease items that require maintenance and sometimes replacement. They are both areas of contention. Neither the landlord nor the tenant wants to be responsible for them because they are costly to deal with. The landlord argues that the maintenance and replacement costs of the HVAC (heating, venting, and air conditioning) unit should be borne by the tenant because that particular HVAC unit serves the tenant's leased premises only. The tenant argues that the roof and its repair and replacement should be borne by the landlord because it is part of the building envelope, and the building envelope is the responsibility of the landlord.

These two items are commonly negotiated. Here are some of the ways they can be dealt with. If the existing HVAC unit is old and needs to be replaced, the landlord may agree to replace it with a new one. At this point, the tenant needs to ensure that the HVAC capacity is adequate for the tenant's use. If the existing unit provides 10 tons of cooling, and the tenant needs 15 tons, the landlord needs to be aware of this before placing the order for the new unit. Once the landlord has paid to install a brand new unit, then the tenant will be responsible for its maintenance and repair, and sometimes even replacement, if the tenant stays there that long. The lease commonly requires the tenant to hire a professional company to maintain the HVAC unit on a monthly basis.

I recently did a deal where the landlord was agreeing to replace the HVAC unit but was stalling on signing the agreement to lease because they did not know the cost of the new, higher capacity unit and whether they would have to provide extra roof reinforcement to sustain the weight of the new unit. The tenant wanted the space and was confident that the new HVAC unit was not going to require additional roof reinforcement. So, in order to get the deal finished, the tenant suggested that the landlord's contribution be limited to a maximum of $15,000.00. If there were any more costs, the tenant would be responsible. The landlord agreed, and we were able to get the deal done.

The repair and replacement of the roof is another bone of contention. Commonly, the landlord will pay for roof repairs and then charge it back to all the tenants proportionally by adding it to Common Area Maintenance charges. Some of the larger, more powerful tenants disallow the landlord from adding roof repairs to their CAM charges. The tenant may agree to contribute to roof repairs but only to a maximum amount, and only on the roof repairs that cover the tenant's leased premises.

HVAC (heating, venting, air conditioning) units on a commercial rooftop

To see a full color photograph, go to www.thedragonbooks.com

Chapter 6

Construction & Other Causes of Heart Failure

Landlord's Work & Tenant's Work

Prior to generating your offer to lease, it is necessary to get inside the space for an inspection. You or your agent can arrange for this by contacting the landlord or the listing brokerage, if the space is listed. Bring your contractor and your designer with you. The premises will either be in raw condition (never previously built out), vanilla shell (the landlord has installed a transformer and electrical panel, dry wall, and stubbed up plumbing), or it will have the previous tenant's leasehold improvements still in place. Look for the following to ensure adequacy for your use:

- The breaker panel: you need to know the capacity of power your business will require
- Plumbing (where and how much): if you are building a medical clinic, you will need a sink in each operatory; if you are building a restaurant, you will need plumbing in several different areas
- HVAC: this is your Heating, Venting, and Air Conditioning unit that in a typical retail space is mounted on the roof above your leased premises and normally serves your space alone.

You need to know its capacity or tonnage to ensure it is adequate for your use. Look for more about HVAC later in this chapter.

- Walls: in most cases, you will want them dry walled, taped, sanded, and ready for paint. Try to get the landlord to remove any walls that you cannot use. If you need peace and quiet, you may want the landlord to soundproof the walls for you; also, if you are building a restaurant, you will need 2-hour fire rating. Ensure that your walls go all the way up to the underside of the roof deck. Your contractor should be aware of the building code for your area.

- Floors: if you can live with the flooring that was left by the previous tenant, that's a nice cost savings for you. Unfortunately, that is seldom the case. If the existing flooring is ceramic tile, try to get its removal as part of *Landlord's Work*, and ensure in your offer that the floor will be "ground smooth and ready to receive *Tenant's* flooring." Then you may be able to avoid the costs for grinding off old tile, grout, and glue, etc.

- Doors and Windows: depending upon the age of the building, they may need to be replaced. Look for cracks in the glass, doors that no longer swing evenly, and hardware that needs replacing; these are all things that can be included in *Landlord's Work*.

- Sprinkler systems: depending on your planned ceiling design, you may have to have sprinkler heads adjusted. Even if your ceiling is to be an open concept, the building code may require the heads to be at a different height than they are now.

Your inspection should include anything that will be important to your operations. Processes such as receiving, and garbage removal, need to be addressed. If you require truck level loading, look at the access corridor (if there is one) to ensure it is wide enough for your pallets and lifter. If you have not included this level of detail in your business plan, sit down with your contractor and write it in with costs. Once the clock starts ticking on your gross rent-free fixturing period, you will be rushed to make some important decisions.

Design, Materials and Finishes

If you are a franchisee, opening a franchised business, many of the decisions herein will have been made for you. Some franchisors simply have you send the Computer Aided Drawing (CAD) file of your leased premises to the home office, and the designers there will create your design drawings and provide a materials schedule for your contractor.

If, however, you are creating your own concept, spend time with your designer looking at materials and costs. Sometimes there are ways to create a certain look with much less expensive materials. But be forewarned, commercial grade materials are designed to withstand much more punishment than materials often used in residential construction. Go back to the WOW Factor in Chapter 3 and be sure to have your designer create a stunning artist's rendering of your design concept, including an exterior storefront elevation, a floor plan, and an interior elevation. Don't worry about the exact square footage; this is a prototype design, the first of 5,000.

Drawings, Permits and Approvals

The first set of drawings you will need are the premises drawings from the landlord. The landlord may or may not have *as-built* drawings of the space. In that case, you may have to pay to have a set created for you. Regardless, you will need the drawings. As-built drawings are ideal because your designer will be able to know, for example, where the plumbing is located under the floor. The goal is to save you money and get your space built on time and on budget. Once your drawings have been created, they will require review by an architect and receive the architect's stamp before they can be submitted to the building department of the municipality for building permit. This process can take up to 2 months or more depending upon the complexity of the project. Do not forget that you may also need the landlord's approval of your drawings, so you should do that step first before making application for your building permit.

Contractors (like lawyers and realtors, are not all the same)

The degree of knowledge and experience of your design and construction team will make a huge difference at this stage of the game. If you decided to hire your brother-in-law that renovates basements in his spare time, you may find yourself in trouble. Trouble means delays and additional costs for you. It may also result in penalties if the building code has been ignored. Take the time to research commercial contractors and be sure to get three quotes before choosing your General Contractor.

Ideally, you should hire a great project manager whose job it is to save you money and get the job done. They are the ones that hire the contractors, control the costs and timing, and report to you every few days. When there is an angry call from the landlord because of an error or omission, the project manager deals with it, not you.

By choosing the right project management group, the money they will save you should be more than justified by cost efficiencies due to good planning, the tendering process, cost controls, and opening for business on time or early. In some cases, when you open prior to your commencement date (the date your rent becomes payable), you get to operate during your gross rent-free period. That is a bonus for you and your bottom line.

Tenant Improvement Allowance (TIA)

This is an amount of money, usually dollars per square foot, paid by the landlord to the tenant as a contribution to the tenant's build out. The T.I.A. is paid after all your leasehold improvement work has been completed, the lease has been signed, and the 45-day statutory lien period has expired. The landlord wants to know that you have paid all your contractors and there have been no liens registered against the property for non-payment. The landlord will also want the tenant to be open for business and paying rent. Some landlords will also require that you submit paid contractor receipts equal to or greater than the amount of the Tenant Improvement Allowance.

Do not get too excited about negotiating a great big Tenant Improvement Allowance, however. Just like the bank, for every dollar that the landlord invests in your business, they will be looking for security in the event that things go wrong. So, when you ask about the rent and additional rent for the proposed location, it needs to be considered along with the TIA, gross rent-free fixturing period, and a free minimum rent period (if you can get one). They are all parts of the same package and, when the landlord looks at the overall economics of the deal, they are trying to achieve a net effective rent number. Net effective rent basically means what the real revenue is coming in from the lease, over the term, less the costs of tenant improvement allowance, rent free period, cost of landlord's work, and leasing costs. If the net effective number rent numbers are within a range that the landlord is targeting, you may have a deal.

Opening – Stocked, Staffed, and Ready for Business

This term will be in your lease, and it means basically what it says. It has greater significance when you are an enclosed mall tenant and the landlord is having a grand opening, and he wants all the retailers to be open and operating no later than a certain date. A lot of money and effort goes into your build out, the hiring and training of staff, and the thoughtful inventory mix and visual merchandising of your store. You may be asking yourself, "Who is the landlord to be telling me how to run my business?" It is a good question, and when you are running a well-established brand that the landlord badly wants in their shopping center, you will be the one telling the landlord how it's going to be. The large branded retail tenants understand what they are bringing to the table and dictate not only favorable rents but many terms, such as their exclusivity, what brands of retailers they will allow the landlord to locate near them, walk clauses (in the event they are not happy with the mall's and, therefore, the store's performance), and many other such variables.

Until you have that kind of clout, you should make yourself familiar with the rules of conduct for your mall location prior to signing your lease. If there are some rules that you cannot live with, they will need to be deleted or renegotiated.

Chapter 7

What if Your Business Fails?
How Can You Get Out of Your Lease?

Honesty is the best policy

Once you have signed that *binding* Offer to Lease, or Agreement to Lease and/or subsequent Lease (the long version), you are *bound*; that's why it's called a *binding* agreement.

That's also why it's imperative that you get the right location and lease terms for your business from the outset. There are no practice runs in retail leasing and site selection.

According to Merriam Webster's Dictionary, to bind is to be obligatory, or imposing an obligation. That does not mean you abide by the terms of your lease only if things are going well. It means you are obligated to fulfill the terms of your lease (all of them) on a timely basis.

Having said that, businesses do fail. So, if it happens to you, what can you do?

The first thing you need to do is be honest with yourself. As soon as you start to suspect that you might be headed for stormy waters, call your accountant. Get a handle on your financial situation as soon as possible.

Communication with your Property Manager or Landlord

Don't wait until you're two months behind in rent. Some landlords will have the property manager looking for you if you are even a day or two late paying the rent. She will remind you that the rent is due on the first of the month, not the second, third, or who knows when. Paying your rent late is a good way to get into your landlord's bad book. When you are late paying your rent, a prudent landlord will send you a notice of default letter. You don't need too many notices of default in your lease file before you start to lose some of the rights that you negotiated in your lease. For example, a clause such as your exclusivity with generally start with words something like this...provided the tenant is not in default and has not been in default during the term of the lease, the landlord agrees not to lease space in the plaza to any other tenant whose principal business is that same as yours. The legal terminology is much longer and more explicit, but the above communicates the concept that you could be in danger of losing a significant privilege. Other privileges such as your options to renew could also be threatened.

If you know that you will not be able to make the rent payments, you need to discuss the situation with your property manager or landlord as soon as possible.

Under-Reporting Sales and why that's not a good idea

Retail tenants in enclosed malls are required to report their monthly sales to their landlord as per their lease agreement. Some retailers under-report sales so they don't reach the threshold at which point the retailer is required to pay a percentage rent beyond the base rent and additional rent they already pay every month. There are several reasons why that is not a good idea. First of all, it is illegal. If the government learns that you are under-reporting sales, they will think that you are planning to underpay taxes owed on those sales. Secondly, if the shopping center your store is in is a strong performer, and you do not have an option to renew in your lease, the landlord may decide to say goodbye to you and bring in a retail tenant that can do the sales that will result in rent plus percentage rent for the landlord.

The Midnight Run

This term is what property managers and landlords use to describe a tenant, usually behind in rent, that backs a truck up to the back door of the leased premises, clears out everything possible (stock, racks, point of sale equipment, computers, furniture, anything and everything that can easily be quickly loaded), and moves it all to an undisclosed storage space. In the morning, the mall manager is left with a dark, vacant unit and a big chunk of unpaid rent.

WE DO NOT RECOMMEND YOU DO THIS!

If you choose to do this (or some variation on that theme), you are breaking the law. You are opening yourself up to lawsuits, fines, or even worse. Even if your landlord does not pursue you and your balance owing, landlords communicate and, at very least, your reputation as a tenant will be tarnished or ruined. There are better ways to deal with your inability to fulfill your lease obligations. Below are some suggestions.

All of the suggestions below start with communicating first with your accountant and lawyer, and then with your landlord or property manager. By explaining to your property manager the reasons why things are not going well, there may be ways that she can help—things that you did not even think of—for example, relocating your business to a smaller space or a location where the budgeted rental requirement is lower. Professional, experienced retail property managers have been through this before. I cannot emphasize the importance of regular, honest communication.

The "Control Letter"

This is a letter that is generated by your property manager that allows your landlord to market your leased premises to other potential tenants that might be interested in leasing your space.

If the landlord finds a tenant to take over your lease, you will be given a notice in writing to vacate in a certain period of time (thirty days, for example). This does not mean you are off the hook. If the new tenant agrees to pay rent less than what you were paying, you may be liable for the difference. The landlord may also charge you for the costs of marketing to find a new tenant, or a tenant improvement allowance they had to pay to the new tenant.

The Bailiff

When a tenant is behind in rent, and it does not look like it is going to become current at any point in the near future, the landlord may decide to call the bailiff. When the bailiff comes, he seizes the premises by changing the locks and takes over the personal property of the tenant that is inside the leased premises. The landlord will then decide to do one of the following:

(a) Distrain for rent in arrears
(b) Re-enter and terminate the lease
(c) Affirm the lease and sue for rent in arrears

The Buyout

In some leases, there may be a term known as an *acceleration* clause. It means that all of the rent, common area maintenance, and realty taxes— in other words, the gross rent for the remainder of the entire term immediately becomes due and payable. So, for example, if you have a five year term at $50,000.00 gross rent per year, and you have just completed your third year, your accelerated rent owing would be $50,000.00 X 2 years remaining = $100,000.00 plus tax.

Your landlord expects you to pay all of that rent because that is what your lease says you will do. Once you contact your landlord and explain your situation, they may agree to allow you to buy your way out by paying something less than $100,000.00 plus tax, but it depends upon the market and how long it will take the landlord to find another tenant for your space. They may flatly refuse and fully expect you to pay all of the accelerated rent immediately.

Ultimately, you can't get out of your lease free, but you may be able to significantly reduce the pain. Being open, honest, and humble is always a good way to start when you approach your landlord, if you are in a distress situation. Back that up with a smart lawyer that really understands retail leasing and lease negotiations.

Now, fly into the next chapter where we discuss how to move forward, whether it's your first location or your 100th.

Chapter 8

Your Next Step Toward World Domination

When is the right time for your next location?

When your business can run well and profitably without you is when you will be able to work **on** your business instead of **in** it. Having well thought out lifestyle goals at this point will help you decide your business goals and the direction and speed of your business growth plans. In other words, understanding your "why" will aid you in overcoming some of the challenges you will encounter in the process of executing the "what" and the "how."

It is also important to understand your customers' needs, wants, and desires. If the successful business you have just built is clearly focused on what your customers want and what they like about you, do not lose focus of that. If you are not clear on what it is that your customers want from you or why they like you, get clear! Ask them. Losing your customer focus can happen easily and will be your downfall.

Inconvenience stores

Gary Larson – Inconvenience Stores

The demise of Blockbuster Video is a good example of a company that lost its customer focus. Blockbuster had built an excellent network of stores throughout North America and Europe. The company was profitable. Their site selection criteria had been flawlessly executed and their operations were efficient and nimble. The locations were highly visible, placed in quality retail plazas that were convenient for their customers, near to great traffic generators like grocery stores, banks, and pharmacies. They negotiated hard for lower than market rents, but landlords loved them anyway. They were a clean use (no smelly garbage), their signage was bright, consistent, and always super visible. The stores leased between 4,500 and 6,000 square feet and provided the desirable corporate covenant.

For their customers, the family visit to the local Blockbuster store had become almost ritualistic. Each family member would choose the movie he or she wanted to watch. Then they bought loads of popcorn, candy, and chips, and everyone went home happy. Parents didn't worry because Blockbuster Video never carried pornography.

But there was problem. One of the reasons Blockbuster was so profitable was from the revenue generated by late fees. They knew that by adopting an on-line movie rental system, the revenue from those late fees would disappear.

In 2007, when Netflix approached Blockbuster to begin merger talks, Blockbuster turned Netflix down. They were just about to launch their own on-line video rental program when they made the decision to change CEOs. The new guy did not understand Blockbuster's focus or what was truly Blockbuster's "real business." He changed the game plan and pulled away from their upcoming on-line movie rental program and, within two years, all was lost.

There are many consultants and business coaches available that can help you achieve your vision. Asking for help is not only wise, it can save you a lot of expensive lessons, not only in money but also in time.

If you decide, for example, that you wish to cover your immediate area with six corporately owned (not franchised) locations, each with a trade area population of 50,000, you can easily plot those 6 stores on a map, then run the demographics for a 50,000 population trade area. Depending on population density, you may need to revise your map or simply have an analytics group help you with this planning process.

You would then execute all the steps outlined in Chapter 4. Once you have identified your first two preferred locations, you may wish to generate an offer to lease for each one.

The number of locations you can open at once will depend on how much money, time, and manpower you have to invest. If all your development capital is coming from your personal bank account, building out one store at a time only makes sense until you are ready to adopt a franchise model or financial investors. If you have decided to pursue the franchise model, then once you are ready with all your legal documents and your franchise-marketing package, you will be able to grow your brand with your new franchise partners and their capital contribution. There is much to learn about this process, and this book is not about franchising. It is about knowing how to help your franchisees secure the ideal location in which to operate their new business. Or if you are the franchisee in the process of identifying your ideal site, use this book to guide you.

Understanding your trade area and number of stores/market

One of the great benefits of a couple of years or more experience in operating your business is access to your business data. From it, you will have the ability to know the approximate boundaries of your trade area and how far and often customers, patients, or patrons are willing to travel to get to your location. You will also have been able to collect intelligence on competition within your trade area. It is important to understand natural and man-made barriers because they are defining factors of your store's trade area. Examples of natural barriers are bodies of water, ravines, major hills or mountains, forests, etc. Man-made barriers include major expressways, large parks, bridges, industrial areas, etc.

To see how natural boundaries affect trade areas, please visit the web site www.thedragonbooks.com

Beware of a half-moon shaped trade area. From my experience at Blockbuster Video, we found that when we located a store on Lakeshore Blvd. for example, and ended up with a 180° trade area, sales for that store were generally about half of that of a store with a 360° trade area. We also learned that a customer would not generally cross a major expressway to rent a movie. Those days are long gone, and you will have to figure out how far your regular customers are willing to travel for your particular product or service use.

To see an example of a 180-degree trade area, please go to www.thedragonbooks.com

Once you have decided on the number of stores you would like in a particular geographic area, then you are ready to identify possible locations that meet your site selection criteria.

If you have systemized your business, one way to raise development capital is to sell a percentage of your company. Once again, you will need a detailed business plan in order to have serious conversations with venture capitalists. But if your concept is hot and your business plan is convincing, you will not have a problem attracting investors. When you have a proven concept and can show years of profitable financial growth, there is always investment money available.

Knowing your estimated location count for a market before entering it is imperative. If you look at the map of a city and you can see what looks like three trade areas, you will want to put your location in the best possible site, centrally located to serve that trade area. You also want a reasonable distance between your stores so that sales of store A do not cannibalize sales of *stores B and C*. If you go ahead and put one store in the middle of a three-store market, you may destroy your market opportunity for the other two locations and open yourself up to infiltration by competitors.

To see an example of a three-store trade area, please go to www.thedragonbooks.com

There are many strategies concerning the best way to build a bricks and mortar brand in a new market. For a big city, one school of thought is to infiltrate the downtown core, create brand awareness, and then move outward to the suburbs. The idea here is that the people that work in the downtown core will have gotten to know and recognize that brand, and will also support it when it reaches the suburbs.

Another strategy that was used by a national junior department store chain was to enter very small markets en-route to cottage country (where real estate is cheap), and their customer base grew to not only include the people that live in the small towns but also the people who were travelling from the big cities to their cottages. As the chain grew to larger and larger markets, they realized that they had some brand awareness in the big cities amongst people that knew them from cottage country.

The System is the Secret

If you have not yet read *The E-myth Revisited* by Michael E. Gerber, please do yourself a favor and read it. Gerber teaches us to create our business plan with an exit strategy. A business that is systemized is a business that can be duplicated and sold. Once you have created a written document outlining every process and job in your business, then you will be able to do the same for your site selection and overall expansion process. The act of systemizing your business increases the value of that which you are offering for sale.

One of the most commonly quoted examples of a system that works is McDonalds' global franchise system of restaurants. Many have tried but few have managed to create as consistently duplicable a system as McDonalds. There is magic in a system that allows multimillion dollar quick service restaurants to be run by 15 year olds. But it really doesn't matter if the staff are15 or 75, they will benefit from the same training system that has allowed McDonalds to successfully expand into more than 100 countries worldwide.

Go and visit your favorite chain stores, restaurants, or services. Be unusually conscious and more aware than you normally would be when you are there as a shopper. Ask yourself, what is it that I like about coming here? Why do I keep coming here over and over? Ask yourself as well, what do I not like about coming here? If this were my business, what would I change? Ask the same questions of your family and friends. Become vigilant about customer service and what makes a good customer experience.

Working ON your business instead of IN your business

The process of getting to the point of being able to work on your business instead of in it, is about documenting each and every job and process and having that written step-by-step instruction available in an operations manual. Recently, I volunteered to work in the back of house at a personal development and training event. I was the newest member of the volunteer team and was amazed at the knowledge and experience that the other volunteer members possessed. There were only three people that were paid employees and the rest were volunteers. There was a written manual that documented each process and how the volunteers would support the trainer on stage and the members of the audience. When I saw that level of detail for volunteer positions and processes, I realized the importance of me documenting the paid positions in my own company.

Exercising your Option to Renew

In Chapter 7, we discussed your terms and options to renew. In preparing to exercise your options to renew, you have an opportunity to improve the terms of your lease agreement. The landlord knows that it is cheaper for you to stay in your existing premises rather than to relocate your business. But you also know that the landlord could sit with a vacancy for a long time before re-leasing the space if you decide to vacate.

While I was the real estate manager working for a western Canadian coffee company, I learned how our company dealt with exercising our options to renew. One of our lawyers, located far away at the head office, would speak with the subject location's store manager, the operations manager, the real estate manager (me), and anyone else that knew anything about the subject store. He was looking for dirt. If there were any problems at that site, he wanted to know about it. It was negotiating fodder. Did the location have problems with parking, or were there trees blocking our sign? Did the store have issues with any of the co-tenants? Were any of the restaurants infringing on our exclusivity? He deployed any ammunition he could use to soften up the lease administrator or whatever poor sole was dubbed with dealing with the renewals. He even had me identify possible alternate sites and their respective rents in the event that he had to threaten re-location. This was how he got renewal rents down and managed to leave the landlord feeling grateful that he didn't lose this branded coffee tenant.

Now, I am not suggesting that you antagonize your landlord to this extent. This was a powerful retail tenant, and they knew how to wield their power. I just wanted you to understand what goes on once you become the controller of the big brand.

A Lawyer is a lawyer…and a realtor is a realtor…

By now, I think you are starting to understand the importance of searching for and finding those specialized professionals that have the expertise you will want and need on your team. We at ***www.TopCats.ca*** can help you with that. Just as in the medical field, there are doctors that are heart specialists, skin specialists, or eye specialists. If you had a rash on your arm, you would not go to see your optometrist. I know that sounds ridiculous, but from my experience, when it comes to lawyers and realtors, that's what people do. There are over 45,000 realtors registered with the local real estate board in my city. The vast majority of them are residential realtors. However, with a little research, you can find realtors that have tremendous retail site selection expertise. Our company, Top Cats Realty, for example, does retail leasing only. It's what we do and have done for the last three decades. We do not do office or industrial leasing, and we definitely do not sell houses in our spare time. Every working day of the week, we speak to retailers, services, and restaurant tenants, as well as retail landlords. We are not the company you want listing your home for sale, even though we are licensed to do so. So, does it not follow that in a field so specialized as retail leasing, that you would seek the help of a seasoned professional with retail site selection and leasing expertise?

The same argument stands for lawyers. There are lawyers that have expertise in family law, personal injury law, labor law, and franchise law, just to name a few categories. There is a tremendous amount of knowledge and expertise to be acquired in each area of law, and there is no way that any one lawyer can truly be an expert in multiple fields. Law firms that make their living processing residential real estate transactions may advertise "real estate" as one of their areas of expertise. But don't be fooled; real estate is a vast field and, just because a law firm has a lot of residential real estate experience, it does not mean their expertise includes the specialized field of retail leasing. Look for the **Resources Section** on the web site www.thedragonbooks.com to find expert legal advice where retail leasing is concerned.

Much of what I have written so far, you can do pretty much without any electronic gizmos or high tech gadgets. By using basic common sense in your site selection process, you can learn why one site versus another will be a far better location for your business and your customers. It does not have to be complicated, but it does require some good old-fashioned work, including going to the site, observing what's there, and talking to visitors and other tenants.

So slide right into Chapter 9 to see why e-commerce retailers are opening bricks and mortar stores and what you can learn from them for strengthening your business.

Chapter 9

Why are E-commerce Retailers Opening Bricks and Mortar (Physical) Locations?

Omni channel retailers are winning the retail game

So why are e-commerce retailers now opening bricks and mortar stores? At the moment of this writing, e-commerce giant Amazon is about to open its first ever bricks and mortar convenience store in its home city, Seattle Washington. Here's how it's going to work. Prior to entering the store, the shopper downloads the app on to her phone, walks through a turn style, pops whatever she wants to buy into her bag and walks out. The "Amazon Go" app knows what she bought and immediately sends her a receipt for payment from her account.

The stores are around 1,800 square feet, about the size of a typical convenience store. When you compare that to a modern day food supermarket, they occupy anywhere from 20,000 square feet to 60,000 square feet, or more. Amazon Go will be able to learn shoppers' buying habits and will then sell them stuff with far greater margins than apples and oranges. The current plan is to open 2,000 stores.

Several other on-line brands are now investing in off-line stores to deepen the customer experience of the brand and create a closer or human connection with customers.

"Out of sight, out of mind," continues to be a problem for pure play e-tailers.

Other North American on-line e-tailers, such as a cool eyewear seller and a men's fashion retailer, have both added dozens of bricks and mortar stores to their mix. The eyewear vendor's stores create a fun experience with pneumatic tubes that shoot eyeglasses from the stock room to the sales floor. The stores also feature books on shelves with sliding ladders. The fashion forward men's wear e-tailer calls its stores "guide shops," where their shoppers get to try on a great new look, place the order on-line, and then have their purchases shipped to their preferred address.

A small shop (only 45 square feet) has opened in Sweden at a small town gas station. The shoppers pre-register on-line for making payment, and local farmers have an inexpensive way to sell their produce alongside such staples as milk and bread.

How to drive web site traffic to your bricks and mortar store

Home Depot and a host of other stores now have on-line ordering that allows customers to order and pay for items on the store's web site, and then pick the order up at the store. Retailers with bricks and mortar locations are trying hard to find ways to improve customer convenience but still have the customer come inside the store. It is well known that once you get the customer into the store, there is a high probability that they will make unplanned purchases. Bonus!

Another suggestion is to bring your on-line presence into your bricks and mortar store. By having easy to navigate computer screens inside the store, shoppers can easily see what sizes, colors, and price alternatives are available and in stock—if not at that store then at one of your other locations. In that case, it can be ordered right there and then and shipped to the customer's preferred address.

If you have a bricks and mortar business, but you have not yet developed your on-line presence, you are missing the boat. You need to get into the game. Even if it's just a mobile app. Having a mobile app is like having a beacon. It lets customers find you, know whether or not you are open, and allows them to make a reservation for dinner or book a pedicure. More than two thirds of every shopping trip starts with an on-line search, more often than not, on a mobile device. So, if you don't have an app and ideally a web site, you are not connected to the on-line world.

Imagine the following scenario: let's say your business is a Jamaican take-out restaurant called Jimmy's Jerk. My husband and I are in the mood for a Jamaican take out meal, and we are currently three blocks away from Jimmy's at a coffee shop. We don't know the neighborhood; we are about 45 minutes away from where we live. So, I go to my favorite restaurant app on my smart phone and type in *jerk chicken*. Three pins instantly drop on the map. Jimmy's Jerk is not one of them. Why not, you ask? Even though Jimmy's has been operating the longest and has the best jerk chicken around, they don't have a web site or an app. My husband also goes to his favorite restaurant app on his smart phone and types in the same thing. He sees a list of reviews and notices Jimmy's Jerk. There is no address, phone number, or web site given, but the review is excellent. So, he takes the time to open a browser, types in Jimmy's Jerk, and is able to get a phone number. He calls Jimmy's, finds out that they are open, and gets the address. So, with some extra effort, we were able to find the best jerk chicken place in the area. But how much more business would Jimmy's be getting if it was easier to find? If it had not been for some good and satisfied customer leaving a review, we may not have found Jimmy's at all— too bad for us and too bad for Jimmy's.

Ensure your website is simple to navigate with clear crisp photographs, detailed descriptions, complete dimensions and pricing, sizing, color and slock availability, videos, and even customer ratings and reviews. If you are in the restaurant business, use excellent food shots. If you haven't yet, hire a professional food photographer. Even the best tasting cooking will not attract customers if it looks bad on the web site. Include your menu. Provide the information that potential customers want and need. If your food is spicy hot, provide an indicator of how hot it is. Provide menu items for vegetarians, vegans, and for those who are gluten intolerant or lactose intolerant. Then provide incentives to shop off-line (in your location) with special offers.

Ensure your store, studio, clinic, or restaurant is easy to find. Once your web site is working for you, you will also need a mobile app. On your website, as well as your mobile app, provide basic details including store hours, address, website link, and phone number. And once you have made a sale, continue engagement through social media and email.

The Human Touch and how it makes a difference to Customer Loyalty

According to *Forbes Magazine*, January 4, 2016 issue, "On average, American households are enrolled in 29 loyalty programs, yet they are active in only 12. This 42 percent participation rate will continue to decline if retailers persist in presenting the predictable, one-dimensional model that rewards customers with points and discounts."

Be creative; find new ways to recognize and reward your customers. Last year, my favorite national coffee chain introduced an app and customer loyalty program that allows me to pay for my coffee with the app on my smart phone and collect points for a free, full size drink, or double the points for a bag of coffee beans. Now, that's not new in the coffee shop business, but they had endless problems getting it working. Their customer service really tried my patience. If I were not such a loyal customer (as I have been for more than three decades), they certainly would have lost me. I'll bet they did lose a number of other customers during that process. Compared to their major competitors, their product offering is superior in my opinion. They don't have nearly enough locations, and their service is inconsistent within their franchisee network. They have closed several locations in the past few years, and that is also aggravating because some of them were good convenient locations that I often frequented.

I hope that they are in the process of rolling out more locations because, in order to be competitive in the coffee business, you need to be conveniently located. The super competitive coffee business is a game of locations like none other.

So, if your dream is to build and expand a national or global coffee chain, you had better get really good at real estate site selection and pouncing on AAA sites before someone else does. It seems to me that a customer loyalty program should give me more of what the vendor already knows I like. I want to be recognized and rewarded for my loyalty. If you don't know how to reward your customers for their loyalty, ask them. Conduct a survey, or hire a survey company or the marketing class at your local college to do it for you. Your loyal customers will appreciate that you care enough to ask them, and you will probably learn how to attract and maintain new customers in the process.

Parcel pickup and the fast growing industry of home & office delivery

Due to the accelerated growth of on-line ordering, there are currently many variations on parcel pick-up and delivery options being rolled out. Amazon has successfully completed a delivery test using flying delivery drones in rural England. Canada Post has created a drive through parcel center that offers change rooms for shoppers that order, for example, three sizes, with the belief that one out of three will fit while the other two will be return shipped before ever leaving the parcel center. There are delivery lockers being installed at gas stations and other convenient pick up locations. It remains to be seen which delivery options will dominate.

Real time optimization technology will begin to work for customers right from the moment of ordering. It allows the entire delivery life cycle to be managed from the point of ordering until proof of delivery.

Consumers now want tighter delivery windows, more delivery options, and even installation services. The next generation of home delivery will allow the seller to offer the customer multiple delivery time choices, understanding and knowledge of the product being ordered, where the customer lives, and what services the customer will need when it gets there.

The retailers will know what drivers are available, delivery routes, costs, and time slots available for delivery.

Canada Post Parcel Center drive thru for parcel pick-up

To see the full color photograph go to
www.thedragonbooks.com

Canada Post Parcel Center includes change rooms

To see the full color photograph go to
www.thedragonbooks.com

Broken Mannequin

To see full color photograph please go to
www.thedragonbooks.com

Will fashion retailers survive in the Internet age?

There are some things that we all like to try on before we buy: fashion and footwear, eyewear and accessories to name a few. I am not suggesting that those categories will not change. In fact, they are constantly changing. The variety of technology that is now being employed in the retail sector is significant. Japan is using customer service robots that greet you when you enter the store and lead you to the items you are interested in. Interactive mirrors are being installed in technologically enhanced change rooms. Once the shopper tries on the dress in one color or size, the mirror can change the color from red to black for example, or the size from 10 to 12.

Virtual reality is making a big hit. Shoppers in Asia are able to put on a pair of virtual reality goggles and walk (and shop) in Macy's famous New York department store. When the shopper's eyes focus on a certain item, pricing and information pops up on the screen. A purchase can then be transacted when the shopper nods her head. There is no need to remove the VR goggles.

There are endless new technological innovations coming down the pipe. Some of them will flourish; some of them will not. Remember, the point is **you can't get a haircut on the Internet.** The more we adopt cold technology in our daily lives, the more each of us will yearn for human touch and human connection. Your bricks and mortar business gives you a distinct advantage in that realm. Studies have shown that sales associates that touch their customer's hand or arm during an in-store interaction have higher sales results.

The salon workers where I get my hair cut take the opportunity to massage my scalp when they wash my hair. They do not have to, but it takes them only a few extra minutes and makes my experience that much more enjoyable for me, the customer. They also massage my feet and hands when I get a manicure and pedicure.

Get creative; brainstorm with your team. What can you do to make the customer experience unique, special, and even extraordinary. What can you do to cause your customer to be so ecstatic about your service that not only does she want to tell all her friends, but she is also compelled to talk positively about it on social media? That is your homework, and I challenge you to think outside of the box in creating a truly innovative customer experience regardless of what business you are in. Please email us at info@thedragonbooks.com. We want to hear how you are getting creative and improving your customers' experiences.

Pizza

Restaurants, Entertainment, Services, and Food Stores are uses that need to meet their customers live and in person. The fun of going to a vibrant and diversified specialty food and farmers market is now being replicated in some shopping centers. Grocery stores are now replacing former department stores in shopping centers. Large entertainment venues that were once shunned by shopping centers as "parking lot hogs" are being courted to take over cavernous vacancies left by now defunct department stores. All sorts of services are being pursued by shopping centers given their ability to draw live bodies into the mall. As we have said before, **you can't get a haircut on the Internet.**

Chapter 10 – Bonus Chapter

Commercial Lease Fundamentals

Robert Kligerman is a partner in the Toronto, Ontario law firm of Owens Wright LLP. He specializes in commercial real estate, with a particular emphasis on commercial leasing matters acting for both landlords and tenants and has extensive experience in drafting and negotiating commercial leases and all related documentation for office, mixed use, retail and industrial properties. His practice also involves corporate and business matters. He is supported and assisted by his partners, associates and laws clerks at Owens Wright LLP, a leading commercial, leasing and property development boutique law firm.

New clients are welcomed and can be assisted with all of the legal aspects of a business venture be it retail, high tech, advertising and marketing, distribution or manufacturing. This includes, of course, leases but also incorporations, shareholder agreements, and all other mattes required by a particular business venture.

Kelly C. Laughton

Robert Kligerman
Owens Wright LLP
20 Holly Street, Suite 300
Toronto, Ontario M4S 3B1
(416) 366-6217
rkligerman@owenswright.com

Introduction

The decision as to where a retail commercial business should be located is of critical importance to the new business, which has been the topic of the book which you have just read. The lease of the business premises becomes the legal foundation and, often, the most valuable asset of the new business by securing the exclusive use of a location and, of perhaps equal importance, provides the certainty of knowing occupancy costs, which are the underpinning for financial projections and planning. This chapter will provide assistance in understanding the basic provisions of such a lease.

The Lease

A binding agreement between Landlord and Tenant for the lease of a premises is created when a signed agreement contains the following six requisites: the name of the Landlord, the name of the Tenant, description of premises, rental cost, commencement date and term. An offer by a Tenant to a Landlord for the lease of a premises is most often found in an Offer to Lease or Agreement to Lease. Upon acceptance by the Landlord and providing it contains the six requisites, it becomes a binding agreement. Typically, the Offer to Lease provides for a lease to be entered into, which expands and details the basic provisions found in the Offer to Lease. A practice of some Landlords is to provide in the Offer to Lease that their form of lease, which is attached to the Offer to Lease, is binding upon the Tenant which is contrary to a Tenant's interests. A Tenant should not be put to the cost and exercise of a careful and thorough review of the lease until an unconditional Offer to Lease is in place. The lease upon being signed, replaces the Offer to Lease. Occasionally, a Letter of Intent will be proposed; however, in almost all instances, a Letter of Intent, even when signed by Landlord and Tenant, has provisions that specifically provide that it will not become a binding agreement and therefore should be avoided.

The Tenant and Guarantor

In law, there are only two legal entities: a person and a corporation. A corporation is a "creature of statute" being incorporated pursuant to a statute of a State, Province, or Country. A business name different from the name of the person or corporation (which corporate name well may be a number) is often registered; however, this business name is not a legal entity and cannot be the named tenant in a lease. Almost without exception, the tenant for the new business should and will be a corporation rather than an individual. This provides limited liability for the shareholder-owner and often a lower income tax rate due to the corporation operating a small business. The corporation is often termed a *single purpose* corporation, as its only asset will be the business operating from the leased premises. Thus should the business fail and the corporation default in its lease obligations, there are no assets available to a landlord for damages owing due to the default. Knowing this all too well, landlords will ask for one or more persons to be guarantors of the lease. There are a few strategies that can be attempted if such a request is made. First, identify the corporation as the tenant from the first contact with the landlord. If an existing corporation is not available, shoulder the expense and incorporate, as this may distract the landlord's focus, especially with smaller landlords. If a guarantor is requested, often there can be negotiated a restriction on the guarantee as to its length (the first number of years of the term) or amount (a year or two of rent).

The Term and Renewal Options

Landlords and tenants usually have opposite perspectives regarding the length of the term of a lease and the number and length of renewal options (a *renewal term* is often also called an *extension term*). The landlord strives to have tenants with long term leases. This provides the landlord with the certainty of uninterrupted cash flow for many years. The tenant rather looks for the flexibility of having a shorter term and a larger number of renewal options. Thus, should the location prove to be not as good as had been hoped for, a new location can be found at the end of the initial term. By way of example, if a 15-year period was being considered, a landlord would ask for a 10-year term with one five-year renewal option. The tenant would prefer a five-year term with two five-year renewal options. Also, the tenant may well ask for three or even four renewal options, as having the options provides additional value to a successful business.

New, retail commercial businesses often need considerable work to be done to build out the business premises. The period of time needed to complete the work is often called a *fixturing* period and landlords commonly provide possession without the payment of rent for this fixturing period, with the term of the lease starting after the end of the fixturing period. The length of the fixturing period is dependent upon the extent of the tenant's work, sometimes as short as 15 days or as long as nine months. This is different from a free rent period which is discussed below.

Two of the important considerations regarding options to renew or extend a lease term are: first, the length of the advance notice to be given to the landlord to exercise the option or options and, secondly, the determination of the Base or Minimum Rent for each option period.

Regarding the notice period, landlords and tenants again have different perspectives. Landlords want as long a notice period as possible so that if the option is not exercised, the landlord has time to find a new tenant. Tenants look for shorter notice periods so that the decision to renew or not can be made at the latest possible time. Notice periods of six months or more, or as short as one month have been used, based upon the particular circumstances of the landlord, the tenant, and the leased premises.

The determination of the Base or Minimum Rent for the renewal term is critically important, and this provision in the Offer to Lease needs to be focused on carefully. Most commonly, the provision will provide that the Base or Minimum Rent for the renewal term is to be agreed upon by the landlord and tenant; however, if the provision does not provide for a method for determining the amount if agreement cannot be reached, then the option is not enforceable. Typically, a lease will provide that if the landlord and tenant cannot agree, then the Base or Minimum Rent will be settled by arbitration and provide a basis for the arbitrator to use in fixing a rent (i.e. fair market rental, date for determination, etc.). The provisions of an arbitration provision are beyond the scope of this chapter and professional assistance should be sought.

The Leased Premises

Area

The area of the business premises that is being leased will be defined and described differently dependent on the building, complex or shopping centre where it is located.

The most straight-forward situation is a premises which occupies the entire ground floor of a single storey building. In most instances, the rent is quoted for the entire premises and not based upon its area. The Additional Rent, that is operating costs and realty taxes, will apply to the entire premises, are the sole responsibility of the tenant and does not need to be pro-rated between other tenants.

In other instances, the Base or Minimum Rent is calculated based upon a cost per square foot of the area of the leased premises. As well, Additional Rent, that is operating costs and realty taxes, are pro-rated between tenants based upon the area of all leased premises in the building. Finally, some leases require the tenant to pay its proportionate share of common areas resulting in a *gross-up* of the area of the leased premises, that is the landlord collects Additional Rent on common areas such as common entryways, mechanical/electrical/garbage rooms, interior hallways, etc.

The take away here is to determine and understand the total rent that you will be paying based upon the area of the leased premises. Knowing the amount of occupancy costs is essential both for negotiating rental amounts with the landlord and ultimately deciding whether a particular location premises is simply too expensive.

Other Rights

The description of the leased area can include other rights and benefits such as:
- reserved parking spaces
- the exclusive use of parking areas for customers
- shopping buggy storage areas

- basements, mezzanines, and patios
- rooftops for the use of HVAC, communications and other equipment
- the right to use an area in the parking lot for seasonal products (e.g. garden centre, Christmas trees)
- a no-build area to prevent new buildings which restrict convenient parking or block sight lines to the business premises
- access to and use of the roof for mechanical and/or communications equipment which would include openings in the roof for connecting to the leased premises
- extended hours of operation outside of usual business hours
- access to and use of loading facilities including truck parking

Careful thought should be given so that there are not unexpected costs or disappointment after the lease is signed. Ensure every point is included in writing no matter how friendly or helpful the landlord or the landlord's leasing agent may appear.

Rent

Rent, in most commercial leases, is a combination of the Base or Minimum Rent, plus Additional Rent. Additional Rent is sometimes referred to as TMI (taxes, maintenance and insurance) but that phrase is outdated and doesn't describe the wide range of costs that are often included. Additional Rent is composed of operating costs and realty taxes. The phrases *net* or *net net*, or even *triple net*, are often seen, however they have no definable meaning. You must look to the lease provisions to determine what operating costs are being passed on by the landlord to the tenant.

The underlying purpose for Additional Rent is so that the Base or Minimum Rent does not include operating costs and realty taxes. If the term of the lease was only one year, the Base or Minimum Rent could be added to known operating costs and realty taxes, making a single gross amount, resulting in a Gross Lease rather than a Net Lease. However, operating costs and realty taxes invariably increase and, in a Gross Lease the actual (Base or Minimum Rent) received by the landlord would decrease as those increases took place. Additional Rent therefore, puts the burden of increases of operating costs and realty taxes on the tenant.

Realty Taxes – In jurisdictions where realty taxes are assessed based upon income, the tenant's share of realty taxes is often determined based upon the rent paid per square foot. By way of example, if there were two identical 100 square foot premises in a single building, but with one paying $10.00 per square foot and one $20.00 per square foot, the tenant paying the higher rent would pay 2/3 of the realty taxes on the 200 square foot building. The alternate and more common manner is for a tenant to pay its proportionate share of realty taxes based on area. There are many variations based upon the type of building, such as if the building has mixed residential and office uses along with retail commercial uses.

Operating Costs – Operating costs have many variations that range from the most basic of maintenance and repair obligations where the tenant pays its proportionate share of gas, water, electricity, insurance, maintenance and repair to more comprehensive obligations, including the replacement of roof, parking lot and mechanical systems, building depreciation and even interest on the landlord's undepreciated capital costs. Further, a landlord's management and/or administration fee of 15% of the operating costs and occasionally realty taxes is common. The most important point is to have the projected cost that will be charged clearly stated so that an informed business decision can be made. This can sometimes be found in the previous year's Additional Rent statements prepared by the Landlord. Operating cost provisions are in many instances negotiable.

Free Rent – In some instances, the landlord is prepared to assist a tenant in establishing its new business by abating Base and/or Additional Rent for a number of months. A landlord may also offer the tenant a cash inducement (usually called a Tenant Allowance or Tenant Inducement) to assist the tenant in its initial costs of constructing its premises.

Gross Sales Reporting – Landlords who want to attract tenants may provide an incentive by way of agreeing to accept an amount for Base or Minimum Rent that is lower than the market rate, together with percentage rent provisions, such that the tenant would pay the greater of the fixed lower rate or a stipulated percentage of the annual gross sales of the tenant's business. The written provision in the lease is complicated, requiring an extensive definition of gross sales, reporting requirements, landlord's verification rights and consequences of default. These provisions are also commonly found in franchise agreements where royalty and advertising payment obligations are based upon gross sales. However some landlords will ask for gross sales reporting even without a percentage rent provision. This should be resisted and, if providing such reporting to the landlord cannot be avoided, all associated consequences of default in the reporting obligations should be excluded.

Commercial Condominiums – The lease provisions for a commercial condominium unit are unique. With a condominium, the Condominium Corporation typically owns the structure, which is the walls, ceiling and floor, not only of the leased premises but the entire development, including all lands, driveways, parking lots, etc., all of which are the *common elements* of the Condominium Corporation. The operation, repair, replacement and management obligations are those of the Condominium Corporation for which the unit owner, that is the landlord, pays through monthly common expenses. The tenant's operating costs are often restricted to these common expenses. Thought needs to be given to whether the landlord or tenant pays special assessments should they be levied by the Condominium Corporation. The lease should also contain provisions requiring the landlord to cause the Condominium Corporation to properly maintain, repair, replace and manage the retail commercial condominium development.

Use

Primary and Ancillary Uses – The proposed business use for the leased premises will be included in the lease as a permitted use. The description of that permitted use is critically important and must be described and completed properly. In addition to the primary use, there should be included the right to sell all of the goods and services which may be ancillary to the principal use; for instance, flowers, dry-cleaning and bank kiosks in food stores. Thoroughly think through all aspects of the proposed business to ensure that the use provision does not restrict the operation of the business, present or as best as can be foreseen in the future. For instance, a restaurant use should permit, where applicable, the ability for customers to take out and/or eat in, the sale of alcoholic beverages, the sale of pre-packaged foods, and live entertainment; a convenience store use should permit a food kiosk, automated bank machine, and lottery terminal. Often, uses are described as primary and ancillary and, carrying forward the restaurant example, the restaurant use would be the primary use and the others ancillary. A broad primary use description is best for the tenant, both in the operation of its business and should the lease be assigned. Following our example, a primary use as an Italian restaurant is clearly less desirable than that of simply a restaurant.

Exclusive Uses – Should a multi-tenanted location be valuable due to there being no other similar business, the landlord can be asked to provide an exclusive use covenant whereby the landlord agrees not to lease to or permit any other tenant to carry on the same use. The permitted use and exclusive use covenant provisions are often subject to intensive negotiation between landlord and tenant.

Restrictive Covenants – The landlord, in a multi-tenanted location, may well have provided other tenants with the exclusive right for their business to carry on a specific use. These are often termed *restrictive covenants*, as they are promises given by a landlord to a tenant that restrict the uses that the landlord can permit to be carried on at the retail commercial location. From the perspective of the tenant starting a new business, depending on the laws where the business is located, the tenant's rights are often restricted, even when the landlord breaks its promise and permits another tenant to operate with the same use. It is therefore prudent to consider if an existing tenant at a location being considered could add additional goods or services which would then conflict with the use thought to be exclusive. For instance, an existing hair salon could add children's haircuts to compete with a new children's haircut business, or an existing restaurant could add tacos to compete with a new Mexican restaurant.

Signage

Signage is often critical to a new business and needs to be carefully considered in the lease. In particular:

- the location and size of signs on the façade above the store front
- representation on pylon signs with considerations such as location, size and monthly charges
- temporary signage for the opening of the business

- possible restrictions requiring the landlord's approval of the colours and design of the signs

Default

Default of lease obligations are divided into two types: one where the rent hasn't been paid (a monetary default) and a second where there is non-compliance with other terms of the lease (a non-monetary default). The landlord can take action against the tenant when the time period and/or notice provisions in the lease have been met. These provisions of the lease should be carefully reviewed.

For a monetary default, leases can provide for the landlord being able to act within a number of days (often as few as 5 days) after a payment date has been missed. Default provisions can be drafted such that the period begins either with or without notice to the tenant.

A non-monetary default should always require a written notice specifying the default and often providing a period to rectify the breach (a "cure period").

If there are insufficient monies to pay the rent, it is almost always best to approach the landlord as soon as the problem is known. Landlords are motivated to assist as a failed business is detrimental for a variety of business reasons. A termination of the lease due to monetary default leaves the landlord without rental income and with the tenant and any guarantors being responsible for the payment of rent for the balance of the term of the lease, potentially a very significant amount. If the tenant is a single purpose company with no assets and there are no guarantors, a legal action against the company will essentially have no consequences. Should there be a guarantor or assets having a significant value in the tenant corporation, a recommended direction is to find a new tenant. The landlord will often assist and permit the business to remain open with payment of reduced or very little rent while a new tenant is sought. In this regard:

- a new tenant may be interested in some aspects of the existing business which could be provided at low or no cost

- the new tenant could be provided with a new lease by the landlord or have the existing lease assigned to it

- the rent that the new tenant is prepared to pay may be less than that payable pursuant to the existing lease. In such instance, the defaulting tenant would be asked to subsidize the shortfall, an amount far less than the full rent for the balance of the term of the lease

An in-depth discussion regarding default is beyond the scope of this chapter; however, the law in many jurisdictions is that a landlord may not seize the tenant's inventory and other assets (this is called *distraint*) <u>and</u> at the same time take possession of the leased premises. In most default situations, possession of the leased premises is taken through the changing of locks, meaning that the contents of the premises must be released to the tenant.

Assignment and Subleasing

The tenant named in the lease remains liable through the term of the lease. If the lease is assigned to a new tenant and the new tenant exercises a renewal option, then the original tenant is released; however, if the lease provides for an extension option, the original tenant is not released. With an assignment of lease, the person or company to whom the lease is assigned becomes the new tenant and is directly responsible for all obligations in the lease including the payment of rent. A sublease is essentially a new lease but between the tenant and the subtenant such that the subtenant pays rent to the tenant who then pays rent to the landlord.

Upon the sale of the business in the leased premises, the lease of the premises is assigned to the purchaser. The purchaser becomes the new tenant. Should the business be failing, an assignment of the lease to a new tenant can save the tenant from defaulting in its lease obligations. Often however, a new tenant can only be found for part of the area of the premises or a tenant cannot be found due to the rent being too high. A sublease can be used to lease part of the premises or to provide a lower rent to the subtenant with the tenant providing the shortfall to the landlord, thus reducing its losses.

Most leases require the landlord's consent to an assignment or sublease and provide that the landlord's consent cannot be unreasonably withheld. There are however requirements found in many leases that limit the tenant's ability to obtain the landlord's consent, usually focusing on the proposed tenant or subtenant's financial and business resources and experience.

An assignment of lease or sublease cannot and does not alter the permitted uses in the lease and any new use must be agreed to by the Landlord.

I

Demolition/Sale Provisions

A demolition/sale clause in a lease permits the landlord to terminate the lease in the event of the sale of the building in which the premises are located, or if the landlord has elected to demolish the building and replace it with another development. Thus, the term of a lease is prematurely ended upon the requisite advance notice (often three to six months) being provided by the landlord. The demolition/sale clause should be strongly resisted by the tenant as it permits the lease to be terminated notwithstanding that the tenant may have spent considerable monies readying the premises and establishing its business.

Searches, Registrations and Non-Disturbance Agreements

It is prudent for a search of the title to the property where the lease is taking place to be undertaken before a lease is signed to ensure that the landlord is properly and accurately described, rather than a property manager or other representative of the landlord in the landlord's place.

The search of title will also provide information as to whether there are registered mortgages. The law in many jurisdictions provides that a prior mortgage has priority over a lease such that if the landlord defaults in its mortgage obligations, the mortgagee may terminate the lease. This is avoided by requiring the landlord to obtain a non-disturbance agreement from the mortgagee whereby the mortgagee agrees that it will honour the lease so long as the tenant pays rent.

The lease, or often a notice of lease should be registered on title. This ensures that the lease cannot be terminated by a buyer should the property be sold (subject to the demolition/sale provision) or by a mortgagee if the landlord is in default of its mortgage, provided the registered notice is in priority to the registered mortgage.

Finally, a written report or confirmation as to uses permitted by the zoning should be obtained from the municipality where the property is located.

Insurance
Insurance provisions are probably the most technically difficult part of a lease. The intent of insurance provisions in a typical net lease is that the insurance obtained by the landlord (and paid for by the tenant) and by the tenant provide a complete umbrella of coverage. Care needs to be taken that this intent is accomplished such that neither the landlord nor tenant can sue each other for losses even if one of them (or their employees or contractors) was responsible. Often, insurance coverages, which the lease requires the tenant to maintain, are available

but at a significant cost. An experienced commercial insurance broker is an invaluable resource and should be found and used.

Financing Your Business

In many (perhaps most) instances, financing will be sought for a new business which may be in the form of a bank loan secured by the assets of the business or equipment financing where the loan is secured by the equipment of the business. In the first instance, a lender often requires an assignment of the lease as security for the loan. This would of course require the landlord's consent. For equipment financing, the lender will require the landlord to confirm that the equipment will not be seized should there be a default by the tenant and the landlord's consent to the removal of the equipment by the lender. The lease provisions for both of these instances need to be carefully considered at a very early stage of discussions with the landlord.

Legal and Other Advice

This chapter is not intended to provide legal advice and not to be relied upon for such. You are strongly urged to find a capable and experienced lawyer; however, there a few basic rules to follow:

- Don't agree to anything that you don't understand. Many proposed agreements are often filled with jargon and meaningless language and provisions that has been copied and pasted indiscriminately from other sources with no one understanding the "Frankenstein" document that has been created.

- Take time to make a decision. Although there can be tremendous pressure, business opportunities almost never require an immediate decision.

- Do your own due diligence first, but then ensure that your accountant is pleased with your financial projections, your contractor with the condition of the premises to be leased and of course, your lawyer with the leasing agreement.

An old saying goes that success comes from equal parts of hard work, expertise and good luck. The best of luck with your new business.

Retail Leasing Terminology

Additional rent also referred to as TMI – outdated (Taxes, Maintenance & Insurance) or CAM & Taxes (Common Area Maintenance and Realty Taxes): an amount beyond base rent usually calculated on a tenant's proportionate share that includes reimbursements for the landlord's operating costs, realty taxes, and all other charges to the tenant that are not base rent.

Buyer includes purchaser, lessee and tenant.

Commencement date: the date that the lease term begins (do not confuse with possession date).

Continuous Operating Clause: a lease clause that states the tenant must be open and operating during the entire term of the lease.

Co-tenancy: A clause in the retail lease that allows a tenant a rental reduction if other key tenants or a certain number of tenants stop operating or vacate.

Covenant: an agreement between the landlord and the tenant that binds one to the other for the performance of the terms and conditions of the lease. Often used in reference to the financial strength of the tenant.

CRU: Commercial Retail Unit – a non-anchor tenant in a retail property.

Default: not abiding by the terms of the lease, such as, by way of example, not paying the rent on time.

Distrain: In the event a tenant defaults in the payment of rent, the landlord holds right to seize the tenant's personal property located within the leased premises in satisfaction of the tenant's rent arrears.

Escape Clause: a lease provision that allows the tenant to terminate the lease for various reasons as defined in the lease document.

Exclusivity: a lease provision that allows the tenant to be the only retailer at the subject retail property allowed to sell a particular product or product line. The words *principle business* and *ancillary use* are used for clarity.

Fixturing Period: (CDN) or Work Period (U.S.A.): a period of time that the landlord provides the tenant in order to build the store, often gross rent free and clearly defined in the lease.

"GO DARK" Clause: commonly, in a supermarket chain lease, there is a clause that allows the retailer to close the store, stop operating, and continue to pay rent to the landlord. The results of the retail anchor going "dark" are often devastating to the CRU (smaller) tenants in the plaza. Some larger, savvier CRU retailers have clauses in their leases that say, "If the supermarket anchor goes dark, then the tenant's rent shall abate until such time as the supermarket either reopens or is replaced."

GROC – gross occupancy cost: the ratio of gross annual sales to gross annual rent. The ratio is a different number for different categories of retailers, normally 5% to 12%.

Gross Leasable Area (GLA): the denominator the Landlord uses when calculating proportionate share for operating cost charge backs to Tenants.

Guarantor: a third party whose financial standing guarantees the tenant's lease obligations.

Gross rent-free: a period of time during which the tenant does not pay minimum rent or additional rent.

Indemnifier: A third party that will compensate the landlord for the tenant's non-payment of rent or other loss.

Landlord Work: A schedule of construction items, spelled out in detail in the Offer to Lease and Lease, to be completed by the landlord at the landlord's cost; normally completed prior to the tenant taking possession.

Lease: a signed, binding, written contractual agreement between landlord and tenant that sets out the rights and obligations between both parties.

LC - Letter of Credit: sometimes used instead of a security deposit – a letter issued by the tenant's bank to the landlord's bank to serve as a guarantee for payment of rent and other obligations under the lease.

LOI (Letter of Intent or Interest): a non-binding letter that allows a retailer to express its interest in a proposed location; once received, a landlord may respond with an offer to lease, including the rents and terms of a binding agreement between the parties.

Midnight Run: See Chapter 7

Minimum rent: also called base rent or net rent: the basic rent that a tenant will pay annually to a landlord, usually in twelve equal monthly payments, normally calculated based upon an amount per square foot, rent that is not additional rent.

Minimum rent-free period: a period of time during which the tenant does not pay minimum rent but does pay additional rent.

No Build Zone: a schedule attached to the lease that is a cross hatched area on the site plan often negotiated by anchor stores that disallows the landlord to build any other buildings so as not to diminish the anchor store's visibility or parking.

Offer to Lease (Agreement to Lease): a prelude to a lease, normally a binding agreement between landlord and tenant that includes business terms, use clause, Landlord and Tenant

Work, site plan and any number of lease clauses that may be of particular concern to the landlord or tenant. Often used in Canada, less common in the USA.

Operating Covenant: the minimum number of operating days and hours that the tenant agrees to be open.

Option(s) to renew or renewal option: a lease clause that allows the tenant the right at its option to extend the term of the lease.

Percentage Rent: commonly used in enclosed shopping centers, rent paid over and above net rent, calculated as a percentage of sales beyond a natural or artificial break point.

Possession date: the date the tenant receives the keys from the landlord.

Radius Clause: a circular distance ring from the subject retail property in which the tenant agrees not to open another store.

Remedy: a cure for a default, such as payment of rent when rent has not been paid.

Restrictive Covenant: a lease provision between the landlord and tenant that limits the uses that the landlord can lease to and limits the products or services the tenant can offer.

"Seller" includes a vendor, a lessor, or a landlord.

Tenant Improvement Allowance (TIA) or Tenant Allowance (TA): a financial contribution from the landlord to the tenant's build out costs either as a dollar amount per square foot, a rent-free period, or a combination thereof.

Term: length of time during which the lease is valid.

Triple A Tenancy: a well-known branded retail chain that provides a strong financial entity for signing the lease, known for paying its rent on time, and for excellent operating standards.

Use Clause: a lease provision that defines the products and services to be offered for sale by the tenant.

Vanilla Box: a leased premise, partially built-out by the landlord depending on negotiations between landlord and tenant; could include HVAC, (heating, ventilation, air conditioning), dry wall, concrete floor, basic electrical, basic or roughed in plumbing, rear door and store front. Other terms referring to either no work of varying amounts of Landlord Work include: **"as is, where is, shell, warm shell, and cold shell.**

Bibliography

"Small Business and the Economy." *Small Business & Entrepreneurship Council.* 07 Feb. 2017 Web http://sbecouncil.org/about-us/facts-and-data/

"Archived — Key Small Business Statistics - August 2013 How many jobs do small businesses create?" Innovation, Science and Economic Development Canada, Government of Canada, 03 Mar. 2013. https://www.ic.gc.ca/eic/site/061.nsf/vwapj/KSBS-PSRPE_August-Aout2013_eng.pdf/$FILE/KSBS-PSRPE_August-Aout2013_eng.pdf

"5 Ways Retailers Can Convert Online Traffic to Brick and Mortar Retail Sales" ZOGDigital, Discovery Marketing Blog.2017, WEB 15 JUL. 2017 https://blog.zogdigital.com/2015/07/27/5-ways-retailers-can-convert-online-traffic-to-brick-and-mortar-retail-sales/

Bryan Pearson, 9 things you don't know about Retail Loyalty programs in 2016 Forbes Magazine, January 4, 2016 Web https://www.forbes.com/sites/bryanpearson/2016/01/04/9-things-you-dont-know-about-retail-loyalty-programs-in-2016/#5f586aaf34df